The Way of Love

Also available from Continuum in this series:

Democracy Begins Between Two: Luce Irigaray (trans. Kirsteen Anderson)

Ethics of Sexual Difference: Luce Irigaray (trans. Carolyn Burke and Gillian C. Gill)

The Forgetting of Air: Luce Irigaray (trans. Mary Beth Mader)

To be Two: Luce Irigaray (trans. Monique Rhodes and Marco Cocito-Monoc)

To Speak Is Never Neutral: Luce Irigaray (trans. Gail Schwab)

The Way of Love

LUCE IRIGARAY

Translated by
Heidi Bostic and Stephen Pluháček

Continuum
The Tower Building
11 York Road
London SE1 7NX
www.continuumbooks.com

370 Lexington Avenue
New York
NY 10017–6503

First published 2002

British Library Cataloguing-in-Publication Data
A catalogue record for this book is available from the British Library.

ISBN 0–8264–5982–X (hardback)

Typeset by BookEns Ltd, Royston, Herts.
Printed and bound in Great Britain by
MPG Books Ltd, Bodmin, Cornwall

Contents

Preface

Carrying out the translation of *La Voie de l'amour* – *The Way of Love* – was not an easy task. The book, in fact, does not speak about something or someone who already exists and for whom a language and representations are somehow available, previously codified. Rather it tries to anticipate, notably through a certain use of language, what could or ought to exist as loving between us, to prepare for a wisdom of love between us – a dimension as crucial, if not more so, than that, above all mental, wisdom which Western philosophy has claimed to be. The book outlines another philosophy, in a way a philosophy in the feminine, where the values of intersubjectivity, of dialogue in difference, of attention to present life, in its concrete and sensible aspects, will be recognized and raised to the level of a wisdom. A philosophy which involves the whole of a human and not only that mental part of ourselves through which man has believed to succeed in differentiating himself from other kingdoms. Not yet having reached the stage of thinking and constructing a wisdom of the relation with the other, beginning with the part of humanity that he thought it good to maintain in only a natural state, which inevitably leaves man himself unaccomplished. The original place of the relation between the two parts of the human has to be cultivated in order for humanity to exist as such. This task is still to be fulfilled by us, and *The Way of Love* sketches a possible scenography for it.

For such work, descriptive and narrative languages, those to which we most often resort today, are no longer appropriate. They correspond to something or someone who already exists, and is even already in the past, or put into the past by what is said. The task here is different. It is a question of making something exist, in the present and even more in the future. It is a matter of staging an encounter between the one and the other – which has not yet occurred, or for which we lacked words, gestures, thus the means of welcoming, celebrating, cultivating it in the present and the future.

Meeting with the other, the different, this has happened to us. We were surprised, touched, wonderstruck, called beyond or on this side of what we already were. At least if we were a little attentive. But, most of the time, we did not correspond to the call. Not, to be sure, because of a pure egotism, but because we still lack a culture of the relation with the other. Until today, what we have found is, at best, to integrate the other: in our country, our culture, our house. That does not yet signify meeting with the other, speaking with the other, loving with the other. *The Way of Love* proposes ways to approach the other, to prepare a place of proximity: with the other in ourselves and between us. The book is in search of gestures, including gestures in language, which could help on the way to nearness, and in order to cultivate it.

This implies another relation with language, a relation which favors the act of speech in the present, and not a language already existing and codified. This requirement of *The Way of Love* necessitated certain choices that I indulged myself to suggest to the translators after reading their translation, perhaps more classic than it is now, choices that I am grateful to them for having generally accepted. The text proposed to the readers is thus written with three voices, and even four, the fourth being that of Martin Heidegger with whom *The Way of Love* converses.* I would like to add another voice, that of the reader with whom I try to hold a dialogue, sometimes leaving to the side more conventional habits. It is also a question here of allowing an encounter to exist without submitting oneself or someone else to the past, to repetition. I ask the reader of the text to accept the invitation to listen-to in the present, to enter into dialogue with a thought, with a way of speaking, and to give up appropriating only a content of discourse in order to integrate it among knowledge already gained. I suggest to the reader, he or she, to let the speaking resonate in themselves and to pay attention to the transformation in their own speech. Reading *The Way of Love*, the reader enters in any case into an interweaving of exchanges: the dialogue that the book tries to stage between two subjects, the discussion that the writer holds with Heidegger, the exchanges between the writer and the translators. To limit listening to the text as to a linear message or to codified rules of translation is thus impossible. It would be better to let oneself listen-to without first knowing where and how the reader will be led to correspond to what has been heard.

In order that the reader not come up against some choices of words, believing perhaps that it is a question of a mistake or an inattention on the part of the translators, or even of the author, I would like to comment on some choices that I have proposed to make in the English translation of *The Way of Love*.

First, in the text, the words "speak," "speaking," "speech" will be found where the reader would perhaps expect the more general and undifferentiated "language," which has been kept only to translate "*langue*" and "language already existing and coded." This is a decision on my part and, at another level, a faithfulness to the invitation which Heidegger extends to try to find where we could make an experience of speaking. My way of answering is that, if such an experience can take place in poetic language and in the articulation of thinking and poetic saying, it first of all exists in a present dialogue with an other different from myself. There we can and we must experience what speaking means. There it is incumbent upon us to take charge of the act of speaking without any form or content that could be dictated to us by an already existing language or world. And such an experience of speech, which is irreducible to any other, is related to an experience of listening-to. But here, once more, we would not have to listen to what comes back to us from a language or a world already there. We have to listen to the present speaking of the other in its irreducible difference with a view to the way through which we could correspond to it in faithfulness to ourselves. Thus it is another scenography of the relation with language, saying, speaking which is at work in *The Way of Love*.

Faithful to the teaching of Heidegger in a way but shifting the emphasis into a frame or a space in which Heidegger did not venture, those of the meeting with an other, another who is different while being the nearest to ourselves: the clearing for the advent of a dialogue or conversation between the two parts of humanity in the respect of their otherness to one another. Such a situation leads one to wonder how to choose the appropriate words to translate "*parole*." To be sure, the words selected because of their emphasis put on the present act of the production of language – speak, speaking, speech – are then endowed with a new meaning, or take on again the meaning that they ought to always preserve: present articulation of a meaning that has not yet occurred, directed to the other according to their speech in order to enter into dialogue with them.

Because *The Way of Love* shifts the emphasis onto the present of speech, onto the duality of subjects, onto dialogue, other questions arose about the use of "Being" and "being" to translate "*être*" and "*étant*." How to escape these words in the English translation of a text which converses with Heidegger? In French, the problem is not the same: "*être*" is a verb in the infinitive – to be –, sometimes transformed into a substantive it is true, which does not especially evoke essence, essentialism, essentialization. In my own work the use of "*être*" – to be – intends to say that a human, and more generally a living being, is irreducible to the almost objectal factuality of an "*étant*" – being. "*Être*" – to be –, at least in my text, would express a conscious and thoughtful assumption of the fact of existing, thus an assumption which ought to always occur in the present, and which provides for a bridge between past, present, and future. That would be one of the most important tasks for humanity. I discovered that, in fact, we cannot be – "*être*" (Being) – without such an "*être*" (Being) becoming an essence, or falling back into a simple substance, outside of a being in relation with an other who is different, and first of all with the other of sexual difference. In such a relation, which undoes any fixed essence, or substance, we can have access to our own human Being. I could say: to an existence which would not be a simple passivity, notably with regard to the construction of space, time, and the relation with the other(s). Such a human 'Being' is always in becoming even if it exists, or ought to exist, in every instant. The capital letter of "Being" seems to extrapolate the "to be" from quotidian living or speaking, which does not correspond to the meaning that I give to the word "*être*." To translate the infinitive "*être*" by "to be" was almost impossible in the contexts where the word occurs. The translation by "Being" thus has been maintained, waiting for something better. But "Being" is said for each of the two parts of humanity and for their own world, which clearly eludes the risk of turning back to a unique and set essence or substance, which could be suggested by a capital letter.

Another very delicate question for the passage from the French to the English language concerns the absence of a "*moyen-passif*" – I did not even find a word in the dictionary to translate its meaning – and the frequent translation by a passive due to the lack of an appropriate grammatical form. A really important part of what *The Way of Love* intends to say then gets lost. An encounter between two different subjects implies that each one attends to remaining oneself. And that cannot amount to a simple volontarist gesture but depends on our ability for "*auto-affection*" – another word that I did not find in the dictionary. Without this, we cannot respect the other as other, and he, or she, cannot respect us. It is not a question, to be sure, of extrapolating into some essence – mine or that of the other – but of a critical gesture for a return to oneself, in oneself, a becoming oneself which does not stay in suspension in immutable truths or essences but which provides a faithfulness to oneself in becoming. Such a faithfulness is indispensable for a meeting with the other, a dialoguing with the other, a loving with the other. Without it we fall back into fusion, or into couples of opposites whose relation will be governed by hierarchy, submission of the one to the other, sado-masochism. How thus to express in the English language "*auto-affection*," one of the keys of my thinking but more generally of Western thought from its Greek beginnings? It is necessary to improvise, to try to let be heard and understood the message, playing with the alternate use of the modes without submitting to habits which require that a "*moyen-passif*" be systematically translated by a passive, or a verb which conceals the process of "*auto-affection*."

The grammatical or lexical choices thus are not obvious and often need to go against the more idiomatic choice or stock phrases. In any case, the objective was to suggest a concrete, living context and a present situation of dialogue, notably with the reader. Another example on this subject: when it was possible, the verb has been preferred to the substantive in order to create an actual dynamic in communication, as analyzed in the book itself. It does not suffice, in fact, to speak about the present, it is important to make this present, and the being in presence, exist. And if some lexical choices have generally been respected throughout the volume to secure a coherence and render reading easier, repetitions as such have been avoided. They do not awaken a present attention: to the meaning, to the other, to the world, but rather send it to sleep because of an automatism commanded by the past.

The lexical choices also pose other complex problems. Referring very frequently to bilingual dictionaries – particularly the *Collins-Robert* and *Harrap's* – when reading the translation of *The Way of Love*, and in order to suggest some changes, I noted that privileged connotations of a word differ from French to English. So for key meanings of my text – "*composer avec*," "*pactiser*," "*figurer*," "*recueillement*," "*les mêmes*," "*relève*" (*Aufhebung*), to give only some examples – it is almost impossible to translate the sense that I desire, at least without starting from a French synonym. Which makes a translation difficult lacking help from the writer, who can give information about the connotations that are wished. But even this help sometimes will not be sufficient. For example, the English language – as the dictionary reminded me – privileges the meaning and the syntactic structure in which a subject is in relation with an object, with property as possession, with commerce, negotiation, competitiveness. How thus to translate a book such as *The Way of Love* whose objective is to stage a relation of love and of dialogue between two subjects regardless of any object? I am sure that this sort of message awakes interest in English-speaking people, but how to translate it in their language is not always obvious. And that gives rise to misunderstandings about my work.

Questions are also born concerning the way of marking gender in communication. On this subject, I would first point out that *The Way of Love* wants to outline the frame of a loving encounter, particularly an encounter able to dialogue in difference, the most paradigmatic and universal difference being sexual difference. As this intention is announced in the Introduction, it is useless to insist on secondary choices at the level of gender, which runs the risk of attention falling asleep about what is to be accomplished in the present because of linguistic uses which have almost become stereotypes. It happens that some people reproach me for not using linguistic procedures marking gender that I was the first, I believe, to promote. Inventing new linguistic forms produced an effect twenty-five years ago that is not necessarily the same today, when such a use could serve to caution a formalism without any content, a "political correctness" without working toward some changes. And another thing: the subject cannot change by making only a decision; such an evolution needs years, even centuries. Strictly speaking, there are not yet subjects properly and completely sexuated. Emphasis on gender thus has to be put on the other. And, probably, it is thanks to respect for the other – particularly as "him" or "her," but also as a "them" or a "they" which preserves gender and does not intend to nullify it – that the subject will little by little gain another status. A differentiated way of being toward him, or her, with whom it enters into relation, into dialogue, will act in return on the constitution of subjectivity. A formal and a priori moral code would not be able to realize such an evolution. The reader thus will not find strict rules in the use of "he" or "she," "him" or "her," but reminders of the crucial importance of sexual difference in the putting into practice of a wisdom of love. The reader will also note that "man," "human," or "subject" are accompanied with "he" and "his" or "itself" and "its," "oneself" and "one's" or "their," depending on whether the word signifies a masculine subject or humanity, or, differently, subjectivity in general. As our culture is, in fact, constructed in the masculine, that is to say according to the necessities of a masculine subjectivity, it may happen that masculine subjectivity alludes to every possible subjectivity in this culture and that a woman recognizes herself in such a subjectivity, even if not in the feminine.

One more remark: rhythm, melody, the poietic take part in the elaboration and the passing on of the meaning. Poetry and thought are less separated and inseparable than our culture, unlike others, has generally asserted. And it is all the more true in a personal creation of meaning, a meaning that wants to say she who speaks and to talk to and with the other in the present with respect to the diverse dimensions which compose the human as such: body, sensoriality and sensibility, spirit, soul, etc. To respect the poietic in speaking, its rhythm, its possible melody, going from one language to another, is difficult, almost impossible. The sonorities, the length of the words, the turns of phrase, are different. And errors become possible if the translator alone takes the initiative. Thus I have tried to make heard something of the poietic of the text, with the agreement and the help of its translators.

If someone, with the aid of a magnifying glass, would object that this English version sometimes differs in some words from the original French text, it would be possible to answer in diverse manners. First, the more faithful translation is not necessarily the one which follows the text word by word without caring for the intention, the rhythm, the style, the breathing which animate and support the unfolding of the words. Next, this English translation of *La Voie de l'amour* corresponds to the first publication of the text, to meet with the desire of the publisher and to honor the translators. Reading this translation, I myself made some slight modifications to the French version of the book. It is not always the first writing of an original text which is the best, and to listen to a translation leads to noting a few changes desirable for a better understanding. In any case, we, Westerners, are accustomed to applying our attention to and confronting ourselves with a still coded meaning, often forgetting the poietic, rhythmic, melodic, more generally carnal requirements which ought to take part in the elaboration and the passing on of the sense. In order to talk to the other, to listen to the other, to hold a dialogue between us, we have to again find an artistic, musical, touchful way of speaking or saying and of listening able to be perceived in a written text, then not reduced to a simple assistance for remembering meaning or to some code to be respected.

Finally, and above all, I would answer that the changes with respect to the more classic English version carried out by the translators have been requested by me and made with their agreement. I thank Heidi Bostic and Stephen Pluháček for the time and for the attention dedicated to carry out a first translation, without doubt more literal, of *La Voie de l'amour*. I am deeply grateful to them for having listened-to and welcomed my suggestions about a difficult task fulfilled by them with care, and for having integrated, when they considered it appropriate, the modifications that I suggested. This English translation of *La Voie de l'amour* certainly would not have been possible without each of us respecting the other in their difference(s). No doubt such a gesture is the first step on the way of love.

Luce Irigaray
March 2002
Translated by Luce Irigaray with a rereading
by Heidi Bostic and Stephen Pluháček

* The texts of Martin Heidegger most involved in this kind of dialogue with him are those that compose the French book *Acheminement vers la parole* (Paris: Gallimard, NRF, 1976), translated by Jean Baufret, Wolfgang Brokmeier and François Fédier from the German *Unterwegs zur Sprache* (Pfullingen: Verlag Günther Neske, 1959). The texts which compose the French volume *Questions 1* ("Was ist Metaphysik," "Vom Wesen des Grundes," "Vom Wesen der Wahrheit," "Zur Seinsfrage," "Identität und Differenz") are also particularly implicated, but not only them. The quotations as such in fact belong to the volume *Unterwegs zur Sprache*, from which almost all the texts have been translated into English in the book *On the Way to Language* (San Francisco: Harper, 1971), translated from the German by Peter D. Hertz. The quotations for the English version of *The Way of Love* thus refer to this book. But the French and the English translations of Heidegger are rather different,

particularly concerning certain terms in question in *The Way of Love* such as: language, speech, speaking, word, etc. The references of the writer of the book are to the French or the German version. It thus was not fitting to use systematically the terminology of the English translation of Heidegger because that would have rendered *The Way of Love* not very understandable. In any case, it is a question here of discussing a general position of Heidegger – about the use of language, for example – rather than arguing about the choices of Heidegger's translators. Perhaps that will happen another time. (Note of Luce Irigaray and the translators.)

Introduction

The wisdom of love is perhaps the first meaning of the word "philosophy." In fact, if theology is understood as the discourse on or about God and metrology as the science of measures, why has the reverse order been imposed in the interpretation of the word "philosophy"? And, above all, why has only one meaning been retained: the love of wisdom?

Certainly in the word "zoophilia," to give another example, "philia" is found in the second position, the interpretation of the word being moreover inflected by negative connotations: an excessive attachment to animals, according to the dictionary. In theosophy as well, *sophia* is understood in a quite pejorative sense. Based on the experience of the divine, on inner life, the knowledge of God would be likened to magic, occultism, at best to mysticism. That which merits consideration and friendship when it is a question of philosophy, incurs suspicion, even reprehension, when it is a question of theosophy. Some will object that the first part of the word in "philosophy" is supposed rather to be an adjective while it is probably a substantive in "theosophy." But the reversal of connotations attributed to *sophia* deserves a more profound questioning. And it does not seem entirely unfounded to question the relation between the univocal interpretation of the word philosophy and the pejorative conception of the word theosophy.

With what wisdom is philosophy concerned, and with what other wisdom is theosophy? What conception of reason demands that theology be considered as a good discipline concerning God and theosophy as a problematic approach? Would this be the case if the meaning of the word philosophy remained plural: the love of wisdom and the wisdom of love? This possible interpretation would imply that philosophy joins together, more than it has done in the West, the body, the heart, and the mind. That it not be founded on contempt for nature. That it not resort to a logic that formalizes the real by removing it from concrete experience; that it be less a normative science of the truth than the search for measures that help in living better: with oneself, with others, with the world.

Confused with a conceptual translation of the

real, a formal knowledge, *sophia* is often reduced to a mental exercise, passed on from a master to disciples, of use in populating universities and in having discussions among the initiated but without the impact on our lives that a wisdom presupposes. The presumed friend of wisdom becomes, from then on, one who falls into wells due to an inability to walk upon the earth. His science causes laughter, like that of other sages just as incapable of governing their life and who nevertheless issue words claiming to instruct us on the most everyday and the most sublime. Between the head and the feet, a continuity is lost, a perspective has not been constructed. And the wisdom of which these technicians of the logos are enamoured is sometimes a knowing how to die, but seldom the apprenticeship to a knowing how to live.

Some theosophists, some defenders of interiority, in love with the cosmos, as body and as universe, in love with a divine not reduced to a logos, resist the formal games to which these eunuchs of the heart and the flesh abandon themselves in diverse coteries. They are suspect in the eyes of such theorists, who seem to forget that the most rational knowledge is first mystical – as certain masters too little listened to have affirmed. For lack of taking this into account, knowledge, if it can be submitted to battles, notably with regard to power and appropriation, no longer conveys much meaning. A manner of passing the time, of taking one's own measure among those who are the same, it hardly indicates a path for living, loving, thinking with wisdom. The philosophers of the West are without doubt the first technocrats of whom we suffer today multiple avatars. Including through the destructive confusion between the essences that they have cleverly fabricated and the flesh, the breath, and the energy that we need to live. And if their competence, in particular that which is sophistic, sometimes commands admiration, have they not failed in the task of being masters in thinking? Not simply, it is true. Reading philosophy sometimes stimulates, even cures. Reading sends us back to our daily existence with our spirit a little more alive. A chess match would have perhaps done just as well, and would have created less mental perversity and illusion. It would be a question of a game and not of the truth itself.

Why thus has the wisdom of love and, in part, wisdom itself, been forgotten? Due to a taste for games? The arrogance of whoever masters something or someone? A certain contempt for life and for the one who gives it? All that and many other things. For example, the will or the need to continue to philosophize among men, conversing with men's methods about problems concerning men.

With, thus, a privileging of the object, of the

similar, of the multiple, as the speech of little boys, adolescents, and men bears witness. A privileging that is totally unthought by the philosopher but which constrains him to remain among those like himself without confronting the delicate relational, but also logical, problems that a dialogue with one or several different subjects poses, or would pose. With women, for example. But is it wise to exclude such a possibility? Rational? Or does it result from a fear or an incapacity to enter into relation with the other? Which ends in strange situations. A learned professor from the Sorbonne proves to be a very mediocre life companion: a little boy in love and a lover of boys rather than women. It was already true at the time of Plato's Banquet.

A little irony does not mean a simple moral condemnation. Rather an incitement to open differently one's eyes upon the task of the philosopher. Who moreover claims today to change his mode of doing philosophy, even to renounce philosophy itself. Perhaps in order to remain in the same type of logic? Instead of destroying, sometimes a little blindly, the edifice already begun, why not recognize its partial character, due notably to the one who constructed it? Why not ask oneself about the identity of the philosopher and about the fact that, staying among those like himself, he has not brought into the philosophical domain the values of a different subject with whom he is called to coexist and to dialogue? Why not question the ways of articulating the proper and the near in such a perspective, and the creations of language that they necessitate?

The field of philosophy from that moment on expands. The intersubjective relation finds the place that it deserves: a real which becomes human only by being cultivated. Not solely through the little differentiated belonging to a group, of which animals can give us examples, but through the elevation to a spiritual level of an attraction born from the most natural of the instinct between different subjects. Without for all that wanting to abolish this inclination, as our tradition has believed it good to do, thus missing the most specific task of human being, and cutting truth, ethics, even theology from their basic values.

Not cultivating what he really is, not even recognizing it, has man not been unfaithful to his destiny – to take up a word dear to the sages of the West? Hence the calamities that tragedies and other literary works recount to us? But the masculine subject has also left behind him nature, woman, and even children. His culture amounts to a sort of monologue more and more extrapolated from the real, unfolding itself parallel to this real in order to carve it up and thus dominate it.

This is not very respectful of the other. And it

does not lead to happiness. Neither does it correspond to a human wisdom, but rather to an exile surrounded by fortifications where man takes shelter. One of the instruments of use to him for constructing this enclosure is language itself. Learning to name, to appropriate with words – like little Hans mastering his mother with the aid of a bobbin, asserts Freud – man surrounds himself inside-outside with a world of signifiers which separates him from the real and from all others. At least from those, men or women, who do not speak the same language, who do not share the same logic, who prefer to communicate with someone rather than fabricate objects of which the name will be communicated to the other, even the instructions for use, unless such objects serve as common currency.

Why not name? And not only objects, appropriate in this way to a world of one's own. Naming what we are also is imperative, what we feel, without aspiring to master the whole, without thus mastering ourselves through and through.

But is naming sufficient? Does speaking with the other amount to naming things? Or is a different language indispensable, to which philosophy has given little thought, of which we have hardly any idea? Our rational tradition has been much concerned with "speaking about" but has reduced "speaking with" to a speaking together about the same things. Which supposes a common universe and conversations about a third without real exchange between ourselves. The conversations can even take as an object speech itself, in its cultural specificity for example. But it is not yet then a matter of an exchange between subjects, even if diversity supplies them with an object about which to begin to dialogue.

For such a task to enter into philosophy, it is necessary without doubt to admit that there does not exist a world proper to all subjects: one truth alone, one beauty alone, one science alone. And that diversity takes place not only between cultures but between subjects, and in a paradigmatic manner between man and woman. Objectivity is thus not one and, moreover, the sensible and feelings have their objectivity and are worthy of being thought. Besides, they must be thought so that one can communicate with the other recognized as other. In order for the relation in difference not to fall back into submission, subjection to one sole subject, to values univocally established, each must bring a meaning of one's own into the dialogue. That requires the capacity for objectivizing the subjective – on the level of sentiments as on the level of knowledge –, the ability to say oneself to the other without for all that forcing upon the other one's truth. The ability to listen to the other as well, to hear a meaning different than the one from which a world of one's own has achieved its course.

From the interaction between the subjective and the objective of two worlds, a third arises of which the expanse is generated thanks to the withdrawal imposed by difference. The constitution of such a place, always becoming, calls for a relation between subjective and objective where the one could never assume nor integrate the other because the one and the other are two, and turn round for each subject in the passage from the subjective to the objective, from the objective to the subjective. What henceforth represents the absolute to be attained is the perfection of the relation – never accomplished. Without confusing it, once again, with some horizon defined by death. Or submitting it to a past plenitude or an ideal future, which amounts partially to the same thing. For the vertical transcendence of the absolute – of the Truth, of the Idea, of the Other – is in a way substituted a respect toward the horizontal transcendence of the other which calls for a different discourse, a different logic, a different relation to perfection. The mastery of nature and of the world is transformed into the elaboration of a shared universe. From a solipsistic love, from a certain reason dominated by logical formalism, philosophy passes to a wisdom of love. A task in which humanity discovers a still to come and fuller accomplishment. Never definitive, always under construction. Its decisive instrument is difference itself: this unthinkable of thought, this unthought which traverses human identity. Giving up its artificial and authoritarian unity, human identity finds itself compelled to a cultivation of the relation with the other that it had neglected. The one is displaced from the subject or from the being to the relation between different Beings capable of assuming the specificity of their real, of their world, without appropriating the other.

Where humanity believed to have already completed its unfolding, by accepting being divided into two, it opens the place of its most decisive creation. The world from that moment turns over, not in order to close itself up a second time, not in order to dissolve its facticity into nothingness or to rebuild an indefinitely fragmented universe, but in order to recognize a forgotten difference, the most irreducible difference, that which separates human being itself without a possible overcoming of this division. Thus never a completeness of the One, but constitution of two worlds open and in relation with one other, and which give birth to a third world as work in common and space-time to be shared.

Philosophy then finds itself radically modified, released from intangible essences and more or less magical ontologies. It may again use certain concepts and notions that had become obsolete or taboo. If the human is divided into two, always open and in interaction in its unity, the Being of each of its parts and of their common world no longer belong to a traditional ontology. Ceaselessly worked by the negative because of its duality, it remains linked to the real while becoming always more spiritual. But this spiritual transforms matter without abolishing it. It becomes flesh, the flesh itself becoming word. The one and the other interpenetrate and transmute each other such that the dichotomy between them no longer exists. The fixed polarities of the one, of the One, return to the duality of subjectivities which, with a view to their human becoming and in the name of the wisdom of love, renounce all completed personal fullness in order to work toward a more accomplished advent of humanity. I am not saying that there will be a relinquishing of beatitude but that this happens otherwise: gained but also received from the other, resulting too from the labor of love of which each receives one's part of happiness, of grace.

Philosophy and theology will find in this wisdom of love a possible reconciliation. The divine there assumes an important place as the becoming of the human itself which, through love, transubstantiates body and spirit. And, with them, the spaces where they dwell, that they build. Theosophy regains its merits and, with it, the domains that it was supposed to include: energies of the cosmos, of interiority, of sentiment.

In this world otherwise lived and illuminated, the language of communication is different, and necessarily poetic: a language that creates, that safeguards its sensible qualities so as to address the body and the soul, a language that lives.

Is it necessary for all that to destroy the existing philosophical corpus? Or rather to modify its perspective? To accept that we have, for centuries and centuries, confused a truth of specialists with that of the human itself? Which does not mean that this truth taught us nothing. But that, instead of claiming to impose itself as the sole order possible for everyone, this truth would have had interest in pronouncing itself only in some coteries. That is moreover what it has, in part, always done. Hence its partial, and biased, character?

The Sharing of Speech

On the Way to Proximity

The Western philosopher wonders very little about the relation of speaking between subjects. It is the relation between a subject and an object or a thing that he tries to say or to analyze, hardly caring about speaking to the other, in particular starting from a listening to the other. The word then has to be sought in order to say, but also the silence. In the gathering of the world thanks to speech alone, the other cannot say their own self, and talking to the other has become impossible. In fact, there exist different worlds that require silence in order to say themselves, to hear one another, to communicate between them. So that finding the appropriate words becomes an infinite task and it is not certain that they always refer to things. Sometimes they are simple paths going from the one to the other, which can be forgotten. They convey toward, and the direction to take is then more important than the thing being said.

It happens that speaking is necessary to create the silence in which to approach. But the word is also what is able to incarnate the body and the flesh that one wants to say to the other. Or the flesh in which to exchange with him, or her. Not a part of the body but a flesh that goes beyond the body without destroying it, amputating it: transmuted physical allowing a communication before and after an immediately bodily touching. Words give flesh before entering into corporeal or carnal exchanges: kinds of annunciation in which the flesh of whoever proposes to approach can be heard.

Thus no consumption but the gift of a sign of recognition indicating in a sensible manner the irreducibility of and to the other: through a color, a tone of voice, a tactile choice of word, a simple vibration.

It is not then a question of transmitting an envelope in which a meaning would exist – speaking in a somewhat authoritarian manner, or at least a pedagogical or hierarchical one – unless it intends to annul the two in a supposedly common third, in the neuter, expropriating in this way the relation. It is instead a question of calling for an exchange by making already heard something of what is proposed in sharing, a question of opening some possibility or possibilities leading to sharing.

In what way would the word be more appropriate than music or painting? Because it would escape the objectality of a thing. It would be nothing but an invitation to share. Not yet closed upon some meaning, but opening from the one to the other – a between-two. Not due to ambiguity but because of the proposal of a communion or a sharing in the sensible allowing steps toward the transcendental of the difference between.

Thus not an a priori communication in an already constituted or coded meaning. But the opening and demarcating of a territory that is still and always virgin with respect to meaning, where approach is possible, or not, according to whether signs are perceived by the one to whom they are addressed, and whether they can move him, or her, on the path toward self and toward the other, such a step leading back to a deeper or more blossomed level of Being.

To speak starting from a connivance in the already known or learned keeps away from a communication-between. What is thought to be a complicity is in fact an exile of the one and of the other in a meaning, where a possible approach is stolen away.

To speak starting from the already known also paralyzes the becoming of the one and of the other. Saying no longer speaks, it repeats the said in a new situation, where meaning gets lost. Discourse is often held in this non-sense. Still adapted to needs, at least partially, it no longer keeps any relation with desire, which always requires staying in connection both with becoming and the present – a present in expectation of a becoming that will generally remain without a future because of an inappropriate speaking. In this sense, language as code, philosophy as concepts are deprived of meaning in the present, except the one of instituting a genealogy in which whoever already knows the meaning is the master. But between the master and the disciple – as between the father and the son – there is no real exchange of meaning. At the most, a non-reciprocal transmission of a meaning in part already dead.

For there to be an exchange, it is essential that the other touch us, particularly through words. But we do not yet know this touching with words, except in a mode that reduces proximity to confusion, to fusion. That through which we would like to touch the other while respecting their transcendence is still expressed in a speaking that distances each of us from ourselves and that most often destroys that in which we have been touched. It is all the more true if we have been touched near the source of our Being. If the words that claim to lead to the transcendental are deprived of sensibility, they cannot reach the other in their source, their proximity to self (except by turning this other upside down?). Touching must remain sensuous, join the near, without dissolving it in the surroundings. Touching must reach it and, as a result, close it again, withdrawn. Enfolded in a proper, which does not make it imperceptible to the other but reveals it to the other, while preparing a proximity between us.

An interval must be provided, a neither the one

nor the other where each finds oneself again and finds the other again while avoiding the one simply overturning the other through what is revealed of them. This interval – and this medium – is first of all nature, as it remains left to itself: air, water, earth, and sun, as fire and light. Being par excellence – matter of the transcendental. And if some other can act as a mediator, it does not seem that this can be to the detriment of the mediation provided by the earthly elemental, as a means of return to oneself and to the other or as building material for the path.

To go toward one another requires the elaboration of other space-times than those in which we, Westerners, are accustomed to living. These, in fact, move us away from one another even when we intend to draw nearer. They are evaluated in such a manner that they prevent the approach of the other. Even phenomenology, in its denomination of the phenomenon, does not seem to be a possible method of preparing for the encounter. To be sure, it calls the other's attention to something but this place where the other is called already leads to entering into a dimension foreign to proximity. The extreme of such a process is to designate the other as an equal, that is to say to subject the other to a calculating valuation that makes the other's approach impossible.

This reduction – in fact impossible – of the near to

the measure of a calculation finally leaves proximity without any measure and without any distance. In this way it occurs that proximity becomes very easily subjected to political – or scientific – rules which alienate relations between citizens. Or, that relations between people become so readily subjugated to money. The best measure then appears to be the parental – even paternalistic – relation, which, in fact, does not know a real proximity or approach. Besides the fact that it is calculated in terms of precedence or age, of power, of goods, it is also hierarchical with respect to alterity and does not behave toward the other in a relation of approximation. What results from this is a lack of differentiation between one and another which prevents every possibility and even every sense of approach between those who are different.

The father is a kind of meta-man – God being here the model – at least such as he is generally represented in our culture. Conceived in this way, such a relation is quite compatible with the domination of the world by all the technologies which aim to get a general view of it from on high, the most obvious example being that of satellites sent to observe the earth and its planetary system. This manner of thinking and living, besides the danger that it represents for cosmic equilibria, prevents any approach because of an appropriating mastery of all that which could enter into a relation of closeness.

Does not the definition of a priori common dimensions also go in this direction? How to impose, without pre-established measures, common dimensions – such as those of the fourfold evoked by Heidegger – save by accepting at the very least that they involve different modalities depending on whether the subjectivity is masculine or feminine? But is it necessary to retain them as dimensions defined as such or as features of the human's belonging to the world, which is not the same thing? There is then neither a single round dance nor a single play of the world but a constitution of subjectivities that try to dance or to play together through – and despite – different unfoldings and refoldings. In this sense, an unfolding that would be only peaceful cannot exist, including ecstatically, except as a suspension of the movement toward proximity. Only in such a movement may ecstasy be concrete, giving rise to the world as it is, or letting it be while giving it a horizon where a human can dwell. This silent constituting pause is not without connection to the speaking that has to allow it to be, including through its withdrawal, its partial, thus non-universal, character: appealing for or awakening energy without capturing it with words – naming, appropriating, immobilizing meaning. No saying, in fact, guards in its said the parts of the world in their proximity. Each pronounces a part of it and it is in calling for alliance with the other that a saying is created in which silence becomes essential.

Without doubt, death already exists in the fact that none of us can say the whole of the fourfold, nor even catch a glimpse of it – without having already lost it in abstraction, in a veiling that definitively distances it from a participation in its round dance, in its play. In this case, the dimensions are named but they do not lead into the round dance specific, proper qualities that are necessary to the play in its concrete unfolding. So the one can bring to the sky its height, the other its density and its vastness. The one invites to rise, the other to stretch out while also being lavish with the matter, which permits ascending without abandoning the earth. The transcendental can thus exist – even in a way ek-sist – while remaining concrete, sensible, shareable.

No word can name it once and for all (except by a first name?) nor be totally foreign to it. It is little by little that words can draw near to the transcendental, if they do not close up upon themselves. The transcendental also exists – perhaps? – in the fracture of a word of which each one keeps a part. Meaning is then sensed but never conceived in only one word. A silence, an impossible to say, moves each one toward an unappropriable signification. Too quickly occupying this silence – or the between-two – by a gesture, gestures, risks veiling the meaning of it: between the two something exists that belongs neither to the one nor to the other, nor moreover to any word. And this something must, in part, remain indeterminate.

Communicating, which wants to speak to the other, unfolds starting from this impossible to say. An irreducible flaw in the saying which cannot be treated lightly on pain of speech losing its meaning, and unfolding without saying anything – except a certain forgetting of what should ground.

Speech is always turned toward the other in order to communicate and turns back to oneself without having been able to say what it had to say. If it was not so, the other would no longer remain the other, and the subject would lose an autonomous status. In its turning back to the one who said it, speech attends to what it has learned from the other but also – if it listens – to that in which it failed in communicating. It will therefore be two in different manners, which is not to say ambiguous. The meaning that it conveys becomes deeper and richer through this communicating in which an incommunicable always remains.

Speech thus escapes the calculation that dominates our time. Always open with respect to a unique meaning, always problematic in its reaching the one to whom it is addressed, it can neither seize nor be seized, neither calculate nor be calculated. It is difficult to cut it into words, meaning circulating in a unique word and between the words.

Is listening from then on changed? Less passive in a way, which is not to say less attentive. Would it be more polysensorial? It is more concerned about communicating with the other – and with oneself – than about discovering the exact and definitive sense of a being, to teach to the other.

From the Multiple to the Two

Of course, speaking to many or speaking to only one person does not presuppose the same relation to speech. In the first case, it must convey a meaning in some way closed, in which the speaking subject converses above all with their own self and with speech. No doubt this kind of meaning is the one that the masculine subject has always privileged.

The feminine subject, on the other hand, takes an interest in the relation between two, in communication between people. This subject is thus confronted with a new task as regards the unfolding of speech. And if the linguist Jakobson was able to detect the prevalence of the phatic function in a speaking between feminine subjects, he then compared it with the language of birds without truly analyzing how the development of communication took place at the syntactic and lexical level.

One can likewise wonder whether the absence of transition between the word – all round, closed – that the ancient divinity finds (referring to Heidegger's commentaries on Stefan George's poem, "Words," in *On the Way to Language*) and a lack of word does not result from a non-interrogation about communication with the other in the unfolding of speech.

To the other, it is not possible to communicate a meaning through a closed word. Such a word is always already a testamentary legacy, which is transmitted without serving to communicate with. It is, in a way, an already realized work that does not correspond to the work of a present communication with the other. It can seduce, become the other's property, as it can be that of a people or of a tradition. It is not really shared between two. It breaks the exchange between the one who gives and the other who receives without that pact in the sharing presumed to ground the symbolic order – an object divided in two of which each has and keeps one part of equivalent importance.

The problem, in such a conception of the symbolic, is that the becoming of the relation is not secured. There is a faithfulness to a status that remains the same. In this kind of symbolic, there is no question of becoming nearer. Furthermore, proximity is then defined through an object and not by a movement of approximation between subjects. And this object is already in the past, not in the present or in the future, except in its reconstruction, its reconstitution.

If the evocation of sharing starting from an object cut in two of which each one holds a part thus really suggests something, this does not suffice to account for the possibilities of communicating between humans. Let us say that we barely approach what this communication is. And, in such an approach, it is destroyed as well because the same – in particular as object – is imposed upon the two interlocutors: they are subjected to the same and do not exchange because of or thanks to their difference. They are stuck or stuck back together in the same, just as it happens in collective communication. A same – code, language, meaning – dominates and regulates it.

A saying other than in words would be that of the poet who, having experienced that everything cannot be thus expressed, passes to song (cf. for example Heidegger, *On the Way to Language*, p. 147). To be sure, to sing together is a sharing of breath. Originally, as Heidegger recalls, a sharing of praise.

Perhaps something more or something other: a sharing of desire, of love. A being in communication?

Is going beyond with speech possible or not? Tone, intonation can modify and favor exchange. But is this not still to evade the question of meaning as such? A meaning that is no longer only informing, passing on but also sharing, communication through speaking?

Can such a communication consist of something other than the invention of a speaking appropriate only to those who are speaking to each other, at the moment when they are speaking to each other? Thus an evaluation of space and of time that could not fall under the calculation of measurements external to speaking itself at the moment when it is spoken, and that could not be codified in documents foreign to the saying itself. Only the becoming of the two subjects would testify to the value of the saying – of two subjects in the approach to themselves and the approach of one another.

The saying, from then on, no longer belongs to only one – who, like Nietzsche, could break by speaking it –, it belongs to the two. Each holds a part of the speech generated and unfolded between the two: a saying produced starting from two but which will not be easily divided again, as is the case for the object given as an example to define the symbol. An indispensable fidelity between persons perhaps finds its signification there.

In all of the reasoning, investigations, or commentaries of the Heidegger of *On the Way to Language*, the communication between two does not exist, the words to speak it are still lacking, as moreover in the whole of Western philosophy. Perhaps, the philosopher is on the way toward it when he speaks of a necessary metamorphosis of the saying, for example in the commentary on Stefan George's poem "Words." But this would then signify that language necessarily lies at the very source of poetry – with which it is possible to agree – and this would ignore that it is sometimes impossible for a word to be in accordance with what is to be said. In an exchange between two, meaning quivers and always remains unstable, incomplete, unsettled, irreducible to the word.

In the exchange between two, a certain resignation must exist concerning the claim of saying everything. No one can say the whole without making exchange impossible. The word as such is forbidden to each in accord with what is to be said. For Heidegger it would be a question of reaching, in the relation to the word, an intimacy beyond measure. It is also true that to refrain from a word granted in dialogue is to let an intimacy-between happen, by safeguarding a free space without violating the intimate of the one or of the other. The clearing of language – the vastness – is then built by two. It becomes a place where the intimate is possible with measure thanks to respect for the one or for the other. And also thanks to the renunciation of dominating the "representational rule of the word" (cf. *On the Way to Language*, p. 151).

The highest rule of the word would consist in not appropriating the thing but letting it be as thing. What is sought here is beyond: how to let be the other as other while speaking, speaking to them. Moreover: how to encourage the other to be and to remain other. How to let the other come into presence, even to lead them there, without claiming to be their foundation (cf. *op.cit.*, "*Bedingnis*," p. 151).

Heidegger invokes here the secret of the word, I would think rather – because of a misunderstanding? or because the philosopher stays already and always in the logos? – about the secret of the thing, or of the other, of their resistance to the logos.

Relinquishing would then be recognition and gratitude (cf. *op.cit.*, p. 152). What deepens through the absence of a proper saying according to me – and, according to Heidegger, would be recognition and gratitude toward the saying itself. Secret of the thing and of the other according to me; secret of the word, according to Heidegger. Word called into question by the thing and by the other, in my opinion; thing called into question by the word for Heidegger. Would this not correspond to a fetishism of the word and of language? Idolatry of the means? In place of respect for the matter in which the thing – and the other – is made, matter above all elementary or elemental, open and thus resistant to the form of the idol, which is never indefinite but claims to take the infinite in the finite.

Why is the word called "the remote"? Whereas it is an instrument forged by humans in order to say themselves? *Techné*. "Treasure" being the word to say the unfolding of speech: a meta-speaking more than the elemental matter of which speech is made and whose availability to the transcendental will be lost in an already defined meaning.

The "giving thanks" or "thanks," of which Heidegger speaks, is intended more for the word than for the thing or for the other. Thus the word – as the divine Word – would be the entity that merits us giving thanks for it. And, if it is lacking, the reality of the thing, or of the other, would be lacking. Such would be the secret of the word. In it, does Heidegger not give up the early Greek world and the project of restoring it to which he dedicated himself? Is privileging the word over the real of the world Greek? Perhaps vetero-testamentary – unless the two are less different than what is claimed? And even neo-testamentary, according to certain interpretations where the flesh is subjected to the Word without an alliance between them.

Does Heidegger not go further than Plato in idealism (a word that is not totally adequate here ...) when he submits the thing to the word? Does he not subjugate not only looking but all the senses, in particular hearing, to the power of language? As if the thing could not exist thanks to the perception that I have of it. Thus it is not the thing that depends upon the word. The role of the word would be to convey a real that already exists.

But the philosopher's partner is speech itself – of which he says moreover that it speaks only with itself. Like him, in a way? He interweaves, interlaces with the speaking of speech caring little, it seems, about interweaving, interlacing when speaking with someone, at least someone who is living and present. He is on the way toward the call of speech, not toward the call of another subject. A speech moreover of which the objective is to say "it is," and, in this way, to cause to exist. Not a speech that invites the other to an encounter in speaking – or in silence.

How, in fact, to attempt an encounter with the other if the thinker – or the poet – dwells in language itself? Without resorting to the phatic function of meaning: tautology? Which is neither to exchange nor to dialogue.

The proximity sought by the philosopher is proximity with language or thanks to it, and not with the other and thanks to him, to her. And it is with regard to speech and its interlacings that he speaks of the impossibility of a direct vision – while it appears to me above all in the relation to the other. And also of an involuntary return to oneself, without leaving for all that an "inextricable" circle where speech as information and information as speech mingle, for example. A speech – always already in the past – rules the sense of the circle. Not the subject, who is summoned by speech itself.

In this way of course, speech speaks with itself alone. No one and nothing outside of it dialogues with its meaning: the monologue closes up in a circle. Silence seems from then on impossible, as it is for the other with whom it is not without relation. At least when it is an original or absolute silence – a return to the noises of nature, no more than that. Or a gathering in oneself without any saying?

This initial, or gained, silence safeguards things and the other in their withdrawal – their integrity, their virginity. It lets them be before any monstration, any appearing: left to their will, their growth. The veil of mystery, which then shields them, shelters them in their innocence. It is different from that veil which re-covers them because of their submission, as a thing and as an other, to a language that has always already veiled them. In the first case, the veil is woven of the air in which every living being lies: is born, lives, grows. In the second case, the veil is already an artifice that submits every living being to a same – dwelling and being – preventing it from unfolding in accordance with its roots. The first veil is also related to a voluntary withdrawal in which the subject, if not the thing, would take refuge in order to respect what lives, what grows without claiming to say its Being and assigning a shelter to it. In such a withdrawal, what is still to come from a becoming, particularly of or in speaking, is also preserved. The future is saved – still, partially at least, to be said. Not already trapped in the interlacings of language. If some permanence exists, it is, in part, fluid: it safeguards, and even gives, silence.

To say that the heart of proximity belongs to speech comes down to having already removed it from its carnal touching. It is in a way to have already divided it from and in itself by a weapon, a logos, to have in a way violated it. Imposing speech as the most intimate divides him, or her, on whom it is imposed as the effect of a monologue of the other – or the Other – with self, with the same. Each is thus separated from oneself, and from the other. No more self-touching, nor carnal mystery always and still safeguarded. No more not-yet-manifested, still-to-come animating the quest: for oneself, for the other. Everything would already be said, revealed. Which deprives the subject of the possibility of performing in and through speaking, and of producing a relation appropriate to the transcendental. Life, flesh, the relation with oneself and with the other are already furrowed and seeded by an always already existing logos. Being appropriate to each situation thus risks getting lost in an in-finite tautology: a phatism of meaning that no longer says anything except the impossibility of saying here and now what is to be said. Lost in the interlacings of a speaking already pronounced and programmed, the subject is imprisoned in its information, in its pieces of information, cut off from a natural language that should help them in their becoming human.

To Speak Of or To Speak With?

It is not only the current formalization of language that threatens the language said to be natural, it is also how it is thought to always already exist and impose its norms on whoever speaks. It thus informs, programs the speaker without them having any possibility of questioning it from an outside. It encloses the subject in a dwelling from which they cannot or do not want to leave in order to go encounter the mystery of the other. Each imperceptibly becomes the prisoner of what they imagine to be the instrument of their most radical mastery. The formalization of which they believe to be the inventor and the actor is already a way of reacting toward how a language said to be natural has formalized them.

That this formalization is historically determined, increases the submission of the speaking subject to its order. It is not a question for all that of upholding the hypothesis of a speech in itself, but the possible and necessary creation of a new speaking. That there is some language in which man is always already situated should, through reflecting upon it, allow the subject to invent, at least partially, a speaking of their own.

If this possibility is envisioned by the philosopher for the poet, but in a way dismissed in the resignation that nothing must be where the word – already existing – is lacking, it is not recognized as a necessity for dialogue. Dialogue then is limited to a complicity in the same saying, the same world, and not considered as a novel production of speech determined by the context of an exchange in difference. For such a situation, there is no already existing speech, and the interlacings of the monologue that speech still maintains with itself should preserve an opening starting from which it would be possible to listen to the other as other, as the one whom we cannot appropriate and whose speech we cannot appropriate, while remaining receptive to listening to them.

The gesture then required in the relation to speech would be appropriation to disappropration – that is to say, to appropriate speech to not be appropriating. Such a process demands that the subject turn inward and learn to disappropriate the world. And to appropriate to disappropriation: another opening of the interlacings that speech maintains with itself. Instead of leading the other to their suite in a house of language already built in its foundations, the subject then comes to a standstill in front of the irreducibility of the other. The subject is silent – a silence which is not the one already captured in the unfolding of an existing speech, a silence which suspends this unfolding in order to open the space of another unfolding.

Whoever speaks is then confronted with a triple operation of appropriation. One of them concerns their relation to a language in which they are already situated, the other their relation to the world or to the object they have to name, the third their relation to the other. These operations are not practiced in the same direction with regard to appropriation or disappropriation. Sometimes it is a question of inquiring about language, of knowing how to use it, making it one's own with a certain detachment. Sometimes it is necessary rather to take an interest in what is to be designated in order to be able to name it in an appropriate way: a way that is proper to it. Sometimes it is a matter of being attentive to what is proper to the other without wanting to appropriate it.

Listening in each of these cases is different, as is the relation to oneself that they presuppose. Sometimes the making to which man would be appropriate dominates, or the letting be. Sometimes appropriation is in accord with the intention of the subject, or rather it is listening which must regulate the intention. At other times language or the world as objectivity command appropriating, unless the other does it.

Heidegger does not consider this last possibility. Dialogue with another would take place within the horizon of a same appropriation of the world through language. The existence of a logos, a sort of more or less analogical double of the real, would be common to all men who would receive this gift from History, from the work of a people. That there is not a common analogue for communicating with the other as such inside an epoch of History does not arise for him as a question. The unfolding of speech then would obey another law, a relation to the real irreducible to the constitution of an analogy similar for all, men and women. There would no longer be a possible parallelism between object or world and logos that can be heard by all people. That stage of communication – which is related to a kind of information that the techniques of formalization can grasp and make their domain – becomes obsolete and appears as corresponding to a need to communicate tied to the seizure of the world but not to a saying that lets it and us be.

In our tradition, the highest and most disinterested intention of language would be naming the world and its objects. It is a matter of grasping them in a saying through words corresponding to the Western logos with its conceptual predominance, or of designating them while letting them be, which is nearer to the Eastern language that the Western poet sometimes approaches. Language is the tool, the *techné*, which the speaking subject uses in order to exist in a world, to dwell in it and to continue to construct it as human.

There does not yet exist an inward return of the subject beyond such a use of language, a return which would allow questioning another possible relation to language, thus modifying the status of language and of oneself as human.

Moreover, the word seems the treasure of language, the word in its nominative function. The fact that the verb is the word par excellence insofar as it creates a link, a state, a world ... is not emphasized. The verb as acting on the world, the other, the subject, is not analyzed in its complexity. Its operation of designation, denomination, monstration, is privileged so as to supplant and to cause the forgetting of other possible actions. The verb disappears, fades away, is forgotten in the substantive. Speaking then loses a large part of its creative function in the present. Only the monstration remains, in which man appropriates himself to a linguistic role which limits his identity without totally opening it up.

If man is the animal endowed with language, who could imagine that this property serves simply to express his needs and to name the objects of his world? Does not language have to serve for transforming instincts and needs into shared desires? In that, man would truly be human, in an exchange with other human beings which differs from the relations that the animal maintains with its fellow creatures.

If being on the way to such speaking is not even a concern for man, it is possible to think that the animal is sometimes more advanced than man in communicating with the other – the animal which calls the other through its song for an approach between the two, or which modulates its singing according to what it would say to the other.

That man can defer – which the animal apparently is not capable of doing – does this suffice to indicate a progress? Yes and no, if the deferring takes place as a passage from the verb to the noun, and if approaching from then on becomes making their way toward each other in an already defined sense without any present act of speaking between the two, or if the approach is regulated by a subjection, a tautology to which two subjects agree to conform, finding in that their complicity.

Immediacy has simply been immobilized in a denomination that prevents coming into presence thanks to a current gesture or word of communication. It is not mediatized, dialecticized, transformed into something other than itself in the relation between two subjects. It is suspended in a word that does not represent a dialoguing but a submission of the subjects who speak to one another to a logos coded before they meet.

That the encounter itself can produce a new speech is not really considered by the philosopher, at least the encounter with the other, irreducible to the same in a tautology of meaning. But being on the way to speech is invited to modify its intention and its path in accordance with what an age presents as the task to be accomplished. Here it would be worthwhile to listen to certain words of Wilhelm von Humboldt (cited in *On the Way to Language*, p. 136). "The *application* of an already available phonetic form to the internal purposes of language . . . may be deemed possible in the middle periods of *language development*. A people could, by inner illumination and favorable external circumstances, impart so different a form to the language handed down to them that it would thereby turn into a wholly other, wholly new language." Wilhelm von Humboldt does not therefore exclude, no more than Heidegger moreover, a modification of the use of language such that speech thus becomes other and new.

However, is not making such a task dependent upon a people already to prevent this mutation from being realized in accordance with the requirements of a dialogue between two subjects? It is in any case not to envision this possibility, nor to accept and favor a transformation of speaking coming from this key situation of its production. Furthermore, the collective subject, the "people," evolves only slowly at the creative level. It will reflect more easily and rapidly the negative and reactive effects of an epoch – technological, for example – than the creative efforts for an intersubjective dialogue.

Nevertheless is it not at this level that technical imperialism – to limit ourselves to a current preoccupation – could find a corrective that allows it to deploy productions favorable to human becoming without being what paralyzes, even annihilates, this becoming?

Could not the current risks of technology, notably in the form of computers, for unearthing a truly human speaking be avoided through the unfolding of a dialogue between human subjects? In this direction, we have progressed very little for centuries, but the multicultural imperatives of our age as well as the discoveries of the human sciences can work toward orienting the development of language in this way. How will we respond, or correspond, to the challenges of globalization, if not through the invention of another language? Through making our way toward finding a language that is more communicative and less subjected to information? Through cultivating the relation between two subjects in the respect for difference(s)? Which allows creating little by little a language of exchange between cultures, traditions, sexes, generations. A discourse or norms already constituted cannot succeed in discovering another speech, in which the subject is situated differently in the use of language. There is no metalanguage of dialogue, no more than there exists a metalanguage of poetic saying.

This new speech brings about, through its saying, the approach of oneself and of the other in a more intimate manner than does the denomination of an object exterior to the subject.

To go in search of oneself, especially in the relation with the other, represents a work not yet carried out by our culture of speaking. It has little investigated this being on the way toward and into interiority, still leaving it to the silence of the without-words, to the night of the without-light, to which the poet at the end of their course, or the mystic on their journey should be resigned. The task of discovering, beyond the customary rationality of the West, a different speech and reason has not seemed imperative. It appears however the most indispensable and the most sublime task for the human subject, the one able, beyond our oppositions and hierarchies, to recast the categories of the sensible and the intelligible in a rationality that as a result becomes more complex, more accomplished for human becoming, and nevertheless everyday and universal.

We enter then into a new epoch of the relation to language. The interlacings of the relation to and of speech are displaced in developing the relation with oneself, the relation with the other. Speech no longer speaks with itself through the objects that it names and the mediation of a subject that has become its servant. It confronts other tasks, where it undertakes to speak what it has left in a still undifferentiated silence or opacity. It penetrates into other dimensions of Being, other spaces and other times, opens or un-covers other clearings where it has to make its way differently.

There no word is yet available, no 'object' constituted. Nevertheless there is not nothing, and silence itself requires being redefined, restructured through advancing into a new speech. If it is indispensable in the relation to oneself, to the other, it has to be re-perceived, rethought with a view to assuring this relational function. It is too mute, materially opaque as long as the subject is not yet on the way to regions of the encounter with oneself, and with the other. Regions scarcely marked out and that it is necessary first, and always, to open up in order to clear them of the obstruction produced by speech itself, and its silences not yet attentive to such dimensions.

Wandering to the Source of the Intimate

Another era of speech is opening. In which it lets itself be put in question with a view to dialogue, dialogues. It is no longer only speech which allots to the subjects, from what is hidden in its interlacings, the task of realizing an appropriate denomination, giving to them and taking from them the word by a gesture alone. Allowing them to live in a world

being already without any possibility of constructing another in which their language-house finds itself questioned, even abandoned, in order to uncover still mute domains of Being.
The subject then accepts being unsheltered. A stranger in his own land, he turns back to a more radical disappropriation, where keeping the senses awake is indispensable for survival. It would be the same in a region of which the culture is still unknown. Here the eyes have another function than that of recognizing the same, the identical – they search for something to eat, for the means to find shelter without yet being able to name. They look at the modalities of meeting with the other, giving information about the gestures to be made without passing through words. They open anew upon the unknown; they show where to go, what to do. They discover again astonishment, contemplation, admiration, restored to the ingenuousness of the child. They see anew, not blinded by what they have to see in accordance with speech.

No doubt a subject will disclose original things to say thanks to this exile from his house of native language. And, if the already known meaning will better appear to him when he returns home, he will above all become able, if he remembers, to say something other starting from and about the human that he is.

Without again falling into information, recital, narrative, forgetful of that irreducible core which constitutes the human itself. A core that no language can claim to have already exhaustively spoken. Of which each language has unveiled a dimension in a culture, while leaving others still silent, notably with regard to the relations between humans, in particular between the sexes.

This place, where what is most irreducible in humanity is constituted, is still to be unveiled and cultivated. Each epoch inventing new masks, new screens, displays, or artifices in order to not advance in this new speech, universal in its diversity.

These evasions in the approach to the human as such go from the privilege of the idea to the reign of fabricating, from the confinement of consciousness in itself to its transfer into the omniscience of a God, from the reduction of the subject in the little differentiated unity of a people to its solipsistic exaltation, from the subjection to a prioris to the submission to a pathos or blind drives, etc.

In what place of culture does one see a man dialoguing with another subject without having first subdued this exchange in some legislating third: the customs of a people, the rules of a language, the formal labeling of objects, a God, etc.? Where has man tried to approach the other through speech without this being already bound in a same that nullifies their differences and reduces their exchange to a tautology, an already programmed scenography, a monologue in two voices? If speaking can then be used to satisfy needs, of what use is it in approaching one another as humans? In advancing toward the unveiling of the human itself?

It seems that man, in the unfolding of culture, of History, has not ceased moving away from himself. He has legislated over the world, particularly with his language, he has explored the interior and the exterior of his horizon, he has even ventured outside his planet and his atmosphere, but, about himself, what does he know? He has fabricated, constructed and destroyed, possessed, but without truly asking himself about what he was as man. Leaving this question and the destiny that it implies to the omniscience or the will of a God, or gods. Without advancing very much in self-knowledge and self-will.

To be sure, laws have been defined with a view to the constitution of the subject and even of his relations with other – but the same – subjects. These laws remain outside the most intimate and the most nuclear of subjectivity. Established through the mental and imposed as neutral and abstract rules that only apply to certain strata of the individual, they do not yet gather into this individual all his diverse dimensions. Which would change the nature and the modalities of enforcement of an order corresponding to the becoming of the subject and of subjective interrelations. Which would also keep this subject anchored to the origin of what structures him, saving for him a margin of initiative, of freedom, of creativity that laws, methods, a prioris imposed from the outside, do not leave him. The possibility of arriving in the present, of being in the present, of being capable of co-presence would thus be favored. A language always already in the past would no longer retain this possibility in interlacings that prevent the subject from situating himself in the present, in the present of presence, and from becoming thus able to adapt to what being with the other in the present, in presence, requires. That is to say, to a being-with different from a complicity and a sharing in an already constituted same. A being-with where speech and thought agree to begin radically listening to and not to lie in wait for new denominations. Such an attitude takes place only at a level of subjectivity, of Being, without then being sufficiently questioned by the irreducible that the other represents. Denomination results from a mastery, even if it lets the thing or the other be thanks to the name given to them. This letting be is a manner of taking them into one's own world, of bringing them under the norms and categories of one's own world.

Thus one speaks of alterity as a category requiring certain moral attitudes. The subject remains then within his horizon, his language, his tautologies, without agreeing to be questioned by an other who, perhaps, dwells in another world. The becoming of human consciousness cannot be content here with condescending and paternalistic or maternalistic attitudes toward the other. It demands letting oneself be questioned turning back to the origin of subjectivity, the entry into the house of language, the foundations of a world. The subject is then sent back to what is most elemental in living and to questioning what living in a human way signifies.

That, in order to delimit this world as human, a Hegel or a Heidegger need explicitly – and other philosophers implicitly – to appeal to death means imposing a solipsistic horizon upon a natural birth and growth and, once again, with the will of mastering the real through a tautology. Where little Hans has at his disposal his mother's presence by assimilating her to a bobbin with which he plays, Heidegger places at his disposal death by assimilating it to the horizon and the foundation of Being. It is always a question of mastering, whatever be the ultimate character of the gesture. Celebrating the life received would allow entering another world where a letting be is more respected. But, as a foundation, the subject then must recognize the other and not enclose the world in the same.

No more simple mastery of the self, of the objects of the world, even supposing some respect, but a letting be that does not impose an already existing language as guardian to life and growth. A letting be that is open – in oneself and to the other – to a still unknown speech and silence. Language remains there a shelter where one can indeed withdraw and even invite the other but not a definitive house for the subject. It is a refuge while waiting to build a more human dwelling, and a common dwelling.

This dwelling cannot be built from words already known by "the twilit norn" (an allusion to Heidegger's commentary on Stefan George's poem "Words"). These words do not yet exist, and they could never exist in a definitive way. It is in a new listening to oneself and to the other that they will be discovered, pronounced. And it is not certain that old gods or goddesses could serve us here as guides. We are perhaps confronted with the unveiling of another relation with the divine than the one that we already know, a divine not only living with humans but in them, and to be greeted and listened to between us. Without immobilizing it, anew, in some limits. The gods are far away from us, it is said. Very far, in fact, when we forget that they already dwell in us and that often we prevent them from speaking: both to us and the between-us.

Let us not expect from them, for all that, already pronounced words but rather the impulse and the strength to pronounce new words that provide in us, in the other and between us a meeting and an alliance between earth and sky, humans and divinities. Sky and gods, in what is most divine in them, are related to breathing and, through the breath, they can communicate with the earth and mortals, dwell in them and among them.

The gods are far away – in us. It is not by searching for them far outside that we will discover them. To be sure, we will perhaps discover in foreign lands traces of gods that we are lacking. But, without a journey in ourselves, to celebrate with them will not really be possible. Approaching gods is not limited to discovering that they exist. It is in the intimate of ourselves that a dwelling place must be safeguarded for them, a dwelling place where we unite in us sky and earth, divinities and mortals. A place where we do not simply invite to come visit us those who dwell far away, but where we discover as proper to us the near that lives in us and that remains foreign to us.

This near does not let itself be named once and for all, so that we could converse about it with others, be they gods. This near is unveiled to us in a dazzling manner but without flashes of lightning. At least its flashes of lightning are of another nature – different from the fire of the sky that strikes Hölderlin. They allow to be glimpsed, while immediately covering over, the opening that permitted manifestation. They do not throw light on something but cast a fleeting glimmer upon still hidden possibilities, which then begin to emerge. They resemble the breaking of the dawn more than the electrical discharge of a stormy sky. Nothing will yet be designated with a name but, from the fleeting illumination, perhaps some words will be born that help to advance into this scarcely uncovered interior clearing. And in which it will not be possible to make one's way without also listening to the speech of the others, human or divine. A word will be retained, for the moment, only if it provides light and strength to approach oneself while meeting with the other. Whose words will be appraised according to the same measure. With the precaution of an additional mystery to be respected, without letting it hinder the proper path.

Which will happen only in a dialogue different from the one that a subject holds with the speech of a people, of a culture. It is on another level of the self and of the other that it is a matter of questioning, in regions not yet said, that it is suitable both to open up and to respect in their virginity, without encumbering them with words that would raise inappropriate limits between oneself and oneself, between oneself and the other. Words then defined to show rather than to celebrate an encounter and a growth that, in part, will remain invisible. Except indirectly – radiation of Being, becoming of the relation, unfolding of a work or of an alliance.

Nothing there that may be said in a decisive manner, stored up like a harvest of words defining the patrimony of a people. Being on the way is more dark, more subtle, which is not to say that it will not provide beacons for other paths. But these paths will not exist without a descent of each one into oneself, there where body and spirit are still mingled, where the materiality of a breath, of an energy, of a living being is still virgin, free from information which has already made any approach impossible. There where it is so difficult to reach, and even more difficult to save something to safeguard oneself in order to preserve a return, an exchange, not submitted to external imperatives again closing the opening, not subjected to an already coded speech that has not made its way into clearings of proximity to oneself, to the other.

Being With the Other

Advancing toward the other is not carried out, for all that, in a blind and mute immediacy. It requires a different way of speaking than the one that we currently know. To become enraptured in a language already there signifies an exile with regard to an approach of the near. More than the adequation of the thing to the word, of the word to the thing, such a path demands forgetting words previously defined, progressing beyond their frontiers and asking language itself how it can allow acceding to proximity.

This will not happen solely through designating the affects by a name nor through limiting oneself to simple interjections, exclamations. Neither will a recourse to the language of a people suffice, except for the relinquishing of singular experience, thus of one's own intimacy – a subjective core irreducible to a collective familiarity.

Making one's way in loving speech cannot be imposed by the history of the loves of a whole people. It risks encountering there more obstacles and paralyses than enlightenments. Besides the fact that love in our culture has been poorly cultivated and not very happy, individual feeling and the approach of the other harmonize with difficulty to collective imperatives coming from the outside. It is neither through fidelity to a tradition, nor by traveling in a foreign land that the path of dialogue will be discovered.

Between a concerted denomination and word-cries manifesting a simple affect, indirect ways of advancing are to be invented. Where the speaking subject was situated and as it were imprisoned in the interlacings of an existing saying, he finds himself in every instant unsheltered by the crossroads where the other waits for him, and by a springing forth of meaning unknown to him. Where language seemed to offer a dwelling for the return to oneself and to the other, it appears from now on as of very little help, often useful for forgetting. From language one can retain some sheet anchors in order to not go down while crossing a ford, some holds in order to avoid a too brutal fall into the abyss, some words in order to escape the dereliction of disorientation. Not very much.

Almost everything is to be reinvented, rebuilt. And, for this building site, what is most necessary is to discover how speech can help to change levels – vertically and horizontally. How to attain in oneself the springing forth of the intimate and how to say it, to communicate it, without obstructing the path to return back to the source? How to listen to the other, to open oneself, horizontally, to the other's sense, without preventing the return to oneself, to one's proper way? What words, not common a priori, will be able to assist, even mark out a path?

The verb will perhaps be more effective than the substantive for laying out traces, sketching perspectives, outlining horizons. The verb of which the act will be sometimes assumed by a subject, sometimes left in an infinitive form – witness to the work of nature or to a still undifferentiated, sometimes common, energy. The verb of which the tense can be modulated: recalling a past, opening a future, remaining in the present or trying to arrive in it, to dwell in it, and which serves to build bridges between different moments, inside a single subjectivity or between two subjects. The verb which can be said in diverse forms or modes: active or passive, interrogative or injunctive, to cite only these examples. And thus bring to light how, already within the subject, an act can be organized in a complex manner. But also how the choice of one's expression can divide subjectivity into two poles: active and passive, interrogating and interrogated, commanding and commanded.

For whoever is not attentive to the use of verbal forms, a dialogue can thus become impossible independently of all deliberate intention. In this lies perhaps one of the reasons which makes our culture more monological than dialogical. Without speaking of the impact of cases on the relation with the world, with oneself, with the other. Privileging the use of verbs which take a direct object encourages the subject–object relation to the detriment of the subject–subject relation, which needs a little more indirection in order to avoid the reduction of the other to an object of one's own. In dialogue, proximity, as well as the proper, are irreducible to a certain form of appropriation – not making one's own is imperative for remaining two. That sometimes demands certain transformations of discourse. "I love to you" is more unusual than "I love you," but respects the two more: I love to who you are, to what you do, without reducing you to an object of my love.

The verb is the instrument of construction of the subject, of the world, of the relation with the other. It marks out paths, builds scaffoldings, provides for transports. It allows expressing personal action or affect but also modalities of relation between two subjects: transitive or intransitive, of dependence or of respective autonomy, univocal or reciprocal . . . "I wash you" differs from "I give to you what is necessary for washing." "I feed you" does not express the same autonomy as "we compare our salaries." "I transmit information to you" is not equivalent to "we exchange knowledge." Not to mention the fact that "I feed you" can mean "I nourish you with my milk," or "I give you something to eat thanks to my work." Two different senses which, in part, depend upon the sex of the subject – a man cannot nourish with his milk and, if he can give birth to an idea, he cannot bring a child into the world. The verb sometimes bears witness to the singularity of the subject more than a substantive can – whatever its linguistic gender, a table (feminine in French) does not have a privileged relation to the feminine subject.

Likewise some verbal constructions will be used more with a masculine subject than with a feminine subject: the reflexive or pronominal form, for example. He washes himself, looks at himself, scratches the end of his nose, buys himself a car, asks himself, etc., more than she does. But this is also true, if not more so, in the words of women about men than in those of men themselves. So that, while a woman talks to or with someone, preferably a him, he speaks to himself or about his work, his projects. That does not make dialogue easy! But consciousness of the difficulty opens the way to new strategies, where each one, man or woman, does not keep on holding monologues in the interlacings of a house of language without wondering if the other hears or understands something in this.

The use of a language is much less neutral and universal than one believes, at least if the subject is not erased, among other things through the denomination, the nominalization of the world. If the subject does not become an exchanger of words, as he is an exchanger of goods or . . . of women. No longer trying to say (oneself), here and now, but to exchange the already said with accomplices of the same linguistic economy, capable of appreciating the surplus value of a word more than what it says of the presence to oneself and to the other of those who are speaking (to one another).

In fact every speaking should always remain unique. Man is "a speaking animal" if he creates speech in order to say himself, to say the world, to speak to the other. The obligation to speak "like everyone else" or according to what has been taught does not awaken, or quench, human consciousness. If the subject does not have, in himself, the source of his movement, he loses his quality as subject. He is a mechanism started up by an energy already fabricated, not free. He speaks but has, as it were, nothing to say that he could say, or no longer has anything to say, paralyzed as he is between repetitions and silence.

The substantive in a way immobilizes time. Time is imprisoned with the thing that the substantive designated in a supposedly immortal or eternal denomination. The substantive represents a kind of ideal in designating, an idea of the thing thanks to the name attributed to it. Once and for all, the thing would merge, for the subject and between subjects, into this often arbitrary word that it has received.

Nothing there which corresponds to a present meaning from the subject, to the sometimes stammering expression of one's own perceptions, affects or desires. Nothing either that permits differentiating the subjects inside a single language but that on the other hand renders them deaf to each other when passing from one language to the other, even when it is a question of the same object, of the same reality. Nothing that can innovate, particularly in the saying of a relation between subjects. The same word submits them, the one and the other, to an already said, prevents them from communicating, themselves and between them, in the present.

A word can be a treasure of which the one passes on the discovery or the knowledge to the other, a work of art that it is possible to contemplate or to enjoy together. But that does not yet mean the two advancing toward the discovery of such a saying. Communion in the already said can even paralyze being on the way toward a saying (oneself or to each other) because of the illusion of a speaking (oneself or to each other) on this side and beyond words: complicit silence, effect of imprisonment in the interlacings of the speech of an other – people, culture, God, some third. This is not to say that nothing will come out of this but that, not taking responsibility in the present for the articulation of the meaning to be said, the subject loses the way to speaking. And his encounter with the other is from then on burdened with centuries of a language that repeats sounds and meanings without speaking in the present. Background noise impregnating even the flesh and preventing it from speaking itself while remaining flesh, and in this way from transforming itself.

Such should be the task of the human as speaking subject. Not to learn to speak an already existing language and to find in it the means for being sheltered, but to succeed in transforming what happens, from within or from without, into saying. Refusing that speech be dictated by a third without coming into presence belongs to the speaking subject as an always present task. It is not possible to learn once and for all how to speak – at each moment the creative work of inventing a speaking is imposed. And if it is necessary here to listen to someone or to something, it is to ourselves and to the one, him or her, with whom we want to dialogue in the present that we have to lend an ear. It is there that a meaning is put to the test of the present of presence. That it sets out, progresses, loses its way, changes in order to start out again, to return to the crossing where the other can be encountered.

And if the other calls out to me, it is certainly not thanks to naming that I will succeed in entering into relation with him, or with her. And it is not a word, which moreover is arbitrary, that will allow me to approach him, or her. Especially since the approach here must be bilateral: I not only have to draw near to the other, we must succeed in drawing near to one another. And the word risks taking from us that space which we must cross little by little toward each other while letting be both the one and the other. If the word delivers a meaning, does it not conceal in its meaning the time and the work of being on the way toward oneself, and above all toward the other? We believe we have approached one another thanks to this supposedly common meaning. We have rather moved away from each other forever because such a meaning does not represent our meaning, that which attracts us to one another – an attraction, a desire, a wanting to do or to say for which we still have to invent the words while continuing to listen to those of the other.

Letting Be Transcendence

The way is thus never covered once and for all. The space becomes settled between the outside and the inside. The distance from the other becomes interiority available to welcome their words. The interval between the other and me can never be overcome. It has to be cleared of a prioris, freed from prescribed or solipsistic certitudes, arranged as a reserve of silence appropriate neither simply to me nor simply to the other, space between us where we are going our way toward one another through the gesture (of) speaking.

This distance is never covered, always to be passed through, and even to be started anew. And the gap has to be maintained. The transcendence between us, this one which is fecund in graces and in words, requires an interval, it engenders it also. The space will be more or less left in its elemental form, the air, or will be more or less woven from the flesh of the one or the other, and from the flesh generated by the encounter. But it is important that an irreducible distance will remain where silence takes place.

It is better that the space which separates us turns back to the materiality of the air rather than becoming an emptiness, where it is difficult to maintain distance for those who feel attraction and where life or breath are in peril. Air is the environment where humans come into the world, where they grow, live and work. It can be inhabited by more or fewer currents or vibrations, but trying to return to the stillness of its expanse is preferable to trying to open an emptiness in it in order to create a still virgin space. Air gives what is indispensable to live, to grow and to speak – to each one, man or woman, and to a relation between two not dominated by the one or by the other. Air allows modulating sounds, speaking with different tones, and also singing, crying or whispering, shouting what seems already evident or keeping the breath for a future manifestation. Air lets someone be in the present, enter into presence in the present, which emptiness does not allow to humans. And sounds circulate in it at a more accessible rhythm and with more agreeable tones than in the ether. Respecting the air between us and drawing from it in the present a part of the flesh of our words grants an approach that nourishes the existence of each one, that allows each to be and to become.

Air is what is left common between subjects living in different worlds. It is the elemental of the universe, of the life starting from which it is possible to elaborate the transcendental. Air is that in which we dwell and which dwells in us, in varied ways without doubt, but providing for passages between – in ourselves, between us. Air is the medium of our natural and spiritual life, of our relation to ourselves, to speaking, to the other. And this medium imperceptibly crosses the limits of different worlds or universes, sometimes giving the illusion of a gained intimacy while we are only sharing a common element. Air can permit us to be in communication if we are going on the way toward each other rather than believing ourselves near because of communion through or immersion in a third.

In fact, we have not yet unveiled our world to the other and proximity is then only passivity or common habits with respect to a world that is imposed upon us.

To approach the other, for two different subjects, does not mean to live in the neighborhood of one another. Then they are barely inhabited by the same things, without necessarily living them in an identical manner. To approach implies rather becoming aware of the diversity of our worlds and creating paths which, with respect for this diversity, allow holding dialogues. Being placed side by side does not suffice for reaching nearness. This local, cultural, national proximity can even prevent the approach because the forgetting of the fact that going the path toward the other is never achieved, requires an unceasing effort and not a standing in the same.

Likewise to enchant the ears of the other by treasure-words or flower-words without doubt comes down to seducing the other through the beauty of a speech but not yet to enter into relation with the other. And to worry about a blossoming of the one and of the other thanks to an exchange that, to each, brings a surplus of life and of breath.

Identity signifies, according to Heidegger, a being the same with itself. This unity of self with self does not persist in an amorphous uniformity; it needs mediations in order to be constituted. It is constructed and not simply received as a whole without flaw.

Where to find what joins this whole? Is it a question of a co-belonging in a whole where each takes place? Mediation would then be what provides for the connection to the whole. But it could also be a question of a belonging of parts to the same, which is different. So, the "to be and to think – the same," attributed to Parmenides, presupposes a belonging of Being and of thinking to a same, that is to a masculine subjectivity. Man's distinctive trait – with regard to the tree, the stone, the eagle, for example – would be to be open to Being as thinking, to correspond to Being in front of which he is situated (Heidegger, *Identity and Difference*, p. 31). Man would be the place of this correspondence. But that to which man in this way corresponds is (only) himself. The Being to which man opens himself, pays attention, corresponds, always belongs to his world. That does not amount to saying that everything in this world is the work of man but that he has appropriated – transpropriated – the whole to himself, or in relation with himself. That there is from then on co-belonging between things and himself.

To experience this co-belonging implies leaving representative thought and letting oneself go in the co-belonging to Being which already inhabits us, constitutes us, surrounds us. It presupposes, in fact, dwelling "there where we truly already are."

But we are then urged to dwell where man stays as a being who dwells alone in the world and not as a being who is in the world in relation with other subjects, subjects who live in another world and who do not necessarily share the same Being. For an incitement to such a task, it is not enough to let oneself be there where we already are. At least not simply. And the modalities of belonging in the same will not furnish the mediations sufficient for constituting or reconstituting the identity of the one, of the other, of the relation of co-belonging. For this relation, it is rather difference itself which will provide us with the necessary mediations. But that implies another mode of thinking than the historical reflection of a Heidegger. A beyond toward which he hints without for all that already situating himself there.

In order to have access to it, man has to leave his own world, or rather to partly open its limits. It is not in his house, including that of language, that he will find how to enter a new historical era, a new speech. The feature referring to the specificity of man has to change place – passing from the relation to things to the relation to the other. It is a matter of discovering in this way a singularity in comparison to the animal, an aptitude – to a great extent still to be cultivated – to found a properly human co-belonging with the other.

If the Being standing in front of me forgets the other's difference, then I am not confronted with the singularity of my own representation and with what it implies for my looking. If what stays in-front-of is only a same unthought as such, I can turn back to my network of interrelations inside of one and the same world. The same conceals the specular or the speculative. I return to myself unchanged in a closed History or world. At least virtually. My ideal image is then deferred into the beyond, into God, which guides my steps toward the different, toward difference, without having any possibility of experiencing it. An end in which I have to believe. If a Being the same and different from me appears in front of me, the relation to Being is no longer situated simply in the same. My own identity is questioned by this same and other in front of whom I find myself.

To suppose Being as the whole of being as ground does not take account of the ground that the relation between human beings represents. This relation does not realize itself as the result of a gathering of human beings, a people for example. It takes place each time between two subjects. For lack of thinking this ground, the relation to God is imposed on us as fundamental cause of unity (and) of thinking – for the world and for man.

The relation between those who are same and different weaves a groundless ground. It corresponds neither to the abyss nor to nothingness but results from an act of grounding which does not end in any ground. The ground is not equivalent then to a multiplicity of interweavings where man already stays and where he dwells – where he is both safeguarded and enclosed. The two perhaps going together for a masculine subjectivity, to the point of having to provide a ground for the groundless through the existence of God, the unique One capable of securing the unity of the whole. Dominating it from an outside and by a capacity to serve as a ground for all relations, being self-satisfying, *causa sui*. God from then on is necessary for the subject constituting himself, and not that toward which he grows as toward a beyond with regard to the indispensable. God programmed by man and not really transcendent to him.

In moving back to the foundation, without doubt it is suitable to go further in order to discover another ground. Is not the interweaving of relations where the subject stays, with regard to the whole of being, already something that subsists of a past relation with that whole the mother was for him, that whole which the relation with her formed?

Would it not be in the place of the ground that the relation with another represents, that the whole of being is arranged? The nature of the relation between subjects is not considered from then on. To be sure, that of the relation with the mother does not yet amount to that of the relation with the other as such. The totality, in the first case, is more present in the relation itself, or in the other. And such totality will never occur as an in-front-of-oneself. The law of the father will transform it into a different totality, cut off from the connection with life and from the relation with the other as living being. The relation with the mother will not for all that be dialecticized, thought. And it will subsist as a ground, an unthought *hypokeimenon* of the subject. Or rather a double ground, which the subject does not yet reach when losing any hold. The constitution of the subject's Being and thinking prevents a return there. It is behind oneself constituted as same that the subject has to move back.

To arrange in front of oneself who or what the

subject is as same, such is from then on the task. What is then reached as ground is a relational world where the other takes a decisive place, an always evaded stage particularly in the onto-theological foundation. Without the mother, there is no engendering, no birth, no survival nor awakening of consciousness. This ground constitutive of subjectivity has remained unthought or reduced to facticity, to the empirical. Now its role, in Being and in thinking, is not nothing, including through its unconscious effects.

"The outcome is the beginning," this circularity dear to the dialectic forgets a beginning. The outcome thus does not account for the totality of the subject nor of Being nor of the ground. An unthought leaves in the dark perhaps the most important part of it: the relation between subjects.

In order to think it, it is necessary to return behind oneself as same, and to consider the first constituting relation of subjectivity, the relation with the mother, where the body and the spirit remain present and often mingled. The so-called law of the father – which acts in onto-theology, particularly through its conception of unity, of Being, of thinking, of the same – will separate the logos from its carnal taking root, and above all from its anchorage in the relation with the other.

It is not a cover over the importance of the

relation with the mother that will permit returning to the ground to which man belongs. And nor can a law regulate, in a manner in fact abstract and exterior to the subject, the relation between humans. Nor the being-together in the same world and speaking there the same experiences with the same words.

It is necessary to turn back to the relation with the mother in order to dialecticize it in a different way. If not, would this relation not be – unthought – that which determines the relation between Being and being, including in its forgetting of difference? Would it not be the relation with the mother which determines the fact of living and even thinking the connection between Being and being as a kind of engendering where the one emerges from the other and the other from the one in a sort of re-covering of all bringing into the world, of all coming into the world? The veiling of this difference – understood here as *Unterschied* – evoking, for whoever goes several steps behind, a will to know nothing of one's own birth. Of the origin of Being as being in-relation-with and as being born-of.

Co-Belonging in the Opening

There exists another relation to the other than the relation with the mother, a relation more specifically human than either maternity or paternity is. These parental relations are indispensable in the animal kingdom as well. Nothing in them is truly proper to the human, except sometimes in certain spiritual connotations that deserve to be questioned. Necessary for the constitution of subjectivity in a certain age, these parental functions perhaps have to lose a little of their importance in order to not prevent a cultivation of the relation with the other considered in its horizontal dimension. It is without doubt there that the most irreducible component of human being should be unveiled in order to allow the blossoming of a becoming which comes with another language.

That implies moving back behind the interlacing of relations between Being and being where the subject stands. Becoming conscious of their substitutive role with regard to a primitive relation with the mother, a kind of Other unthought as such. Behind the constitution of such a world, man finds himself to be again unsheltered from constructions of his historical constitution. Insofar as he can think beyond – alone or helped by an other irreducible to him –, he discovers that his world took little account of the relation to other humans, in any case to those who do not share the same universe as him.

Man finds himself alone on his planet with the desire or the obligation to dialogue, not only with animals or with flowers, but with a princess or with strangers reaching his territory. Everything that was customary or familiar for him, including his transcendental landmarks, proves to be obsolete. And he feels himself to be more alone and naked when the other draws near to him, at least if he steps back so as to be capable of not assimilating the one who comes into his world. Making the one who arrives a simple inhabitant of his planet, a new being in his unchanged horizon, particularly his mental horizon, does not yet amount to welcoming the other. It is rather to reduce the other to the same.

For the welcome to be real, it is important to step back behind one's own horizon, beyond the limit of what was until then proper to oneself in order, beyond the threshold, to question the unknown who comes.

No event more unveiling – for oneself and for the world, for Being and for being – can happen. It is a matter of passing to another look, another light, another relation to oneself, to the world, that we do not yet know. To reach it requires going round one's world, but not by plane, boat, or balloon, all means of transport which partially take the place of a return to the origin of one's own world.

It is not only around the earth that we must turn but around ourselves in order to be capable of opening ourselves, including dialectically, to another who does not have and never will have a site there. It is upon ourselves and upon our world that we henceforth have to impose a negativity and not upon the world which stands in front of us. A new epoch of thinking, of Being requires that all we live as irreducibly proper to man be subjected to the negative in order to take place in another kind of arrangement where to welcome the other and to dialogue with him, or her, become possible.

The unity of the being as human should then be measured with respect to the unity of the relation with the other taking account of difference. Such a unity remains open and leaves to each term its specificity and its autonomy. The unity of the relation between two subjects is a creation, a work of the two elaborated starting from the attraction, the desire which pushes the one toward the other without the relation being then already conceived as a "with the other." The first gesture, the instinctive gesture, wants rather the satisfaction which takes the other as an instrument of pleasure, or even an appropriation that reduces or cancels the two in one of the parts. Which abolishes the relation as human.

For this human relation to occur, it is necessary that we consider its value as both universal and supreme, that is to say as the foremost task of humanity. It cannot be subordinated to any task on pain of fragmenting human being itself, its lone non-reductive partition being: woman and man. If the Being of one of the two elements is taken as the only pole of division, its relation with the other becomes impossible. It will seek in the other the lost whole, the complement of its amputated Being, the instrument of its division or of its reunification. It will claim or believe that a single term is capable of establishing a universal model, this model becoming from then on inappropriate to human being in its totality and, moreover or at the same time, authoritarian and dogmatic.

This unique Being will have then annihilated or lost the being and Being of the whole of the human and of the relation between humans, which require virgin matter or space belonging neither to the one nor to the other but in which the one and the other can enter into presence, each one in relation to the other. What safeguards the between-two as a place available for the entering into presence is the limit that each imposes upon oneself in the fidelity to self and to the space-time open through the respect of the other as such, of their irreducibility.

The aim of thought, its "thing," no longer corresponds to a being, at least a stable and univocal one. It is, at each moment, to be created in a memory of the past and an attention to the present.

It corresponds to the building of a bridge – at the same time practicable and mobile – between two different subjects, each one bringing to it a singular contribution, both proper to oneself and appropriate to the other.

The a priori representation of the work or of the object no longer exists except as an in-front-of empty of content. An intention animates us which is no longer even one. It must, in fact, take account of two subjects and of the relation between them. This intention corresponds perhaps to an assumption of the desire which permits articulating subjective and objective in a relation where each subject constantly occupies the two poles.

This motion is what, in its going and its return, constitutes the subject, marking him with an imprint that he imposes upon himself but in which the other is present. The subject thus no longer has as a principal task to construct a world while impressing his mark upon it. The subject's highest work is to constitute himself as human, to construct the objectivity of his subjectivity as human. This subjectivity is essentially relational. Whoever is capable of providing in oneself a place not only for the other but for the relation with the other is human.

This cannot happen in a pure instantaneousness. An interior reserve is indispensable, a kind of availability to thinking which permits listening, welcoming, and a response respecting the two subjects and their relation. Another relation to space and to time becomes necessary, elaborated so that the human will become from then on sheltered in the work of a becoming human. This shelter is built by the two in the respect for mutual differences, nature being transmuted into a spiritual matter which little by little envelops and protects the subjects on their path while constraining them to pursue it. Human being only exists thanks to a relational becoming which is proper to it, in which it transforms natural properties into spiritual aptitudes, particularly as concerns sexual attraction and procreation. Humanity is composed of only two different beings, a feature that bears witness to the human's aptitude for differing from other kingdoms or species: vegetable, animal, and even angelic.

Co-propriation perhaps has something to do with identity if it is understood as the co-belonging of man and woman in humanity. No longer a question here of the more or less immediate co-belonging of a subject with only a proper Being, but of a link to Being which is dual, including in its foundation, and must remain so. The meaning of "identity" is then modified insofar as it is no longer determined by the same understood as an equivalence between two terms – be they "thinking" and "Being." It is rather the difference between two terms – man and woman – that brings each one back to oneself thanks to the construction of a temporality in which relation to the same does not take root in a tautology but in a becoming. The same, from then on, is not appraised as similitude but as a fidelity to oneself compelled by the care of the human, particularly as care of the other.

In order that the "you" take place in a relation with the "I," the "I" has to secure a faithfulness to its Being in which the other can trust. In the elaboration of its temporality, the "I" must be listening both to the "you" and to the self. Copropriation in the human necessitates a dialogue in which the elements remain two – speaking oneself and to the other and listening to oneself and to the other. Speech does not a priori have to assign to each, man or woman, an identity. This identity has to be built. Being cannot simply be in the past, it is still future. Otherwise the human itself becomes a thing of speech, and of a speech virtually already constituted.

In order to pass from the past to the future, a releasing all hold is indispensable, a letting be. Rather than a diving into the depths, why not envision it as the uncovering, the unveiling of a still closed sky. Or the approach to a world where the co-belonging of earth and sky, of mortals and divinities, is not determined beforehand in its Being. The dialogue between two living subjects opens and closes again at each moment the question of what Being is.

Releasing all hold would no longer take place with regard to the groundless ground of only one subject, a subject who doubles and veils their sameness through the hypothesis of an objective same: Being and thinking – the same. Releasing all hold would be carried out toward a future of which the equation escapes us, and with regard to an other irreducible to the same for each subject. Letting go then gives access to a truly open space-time where co-belonging is still to be created.

Being for man is still without dwelling in what concerns what is most human in it: the relation with the other. To reach this stage, the language which has provided him with a shelter must be modified. Naming or designating will no longer be its principal function but the ability to assure the entering into relation with the other.

I enter into presence starting from myself but also starting from the other. At least if I take account of such presence and do not reduce it to nothing. But the change in my behavior relative to the other can sometimes signify a remaining the same rather than a becoming what I am. To be sure, I am, remain, or become same in a continuity with myself, but also because of the impact of the other upon me, or because of the belief that I have to submit myself to the same language in order to enter into relation with the other. This same from then on paralyzes me, like a fabricated form which prevents the efflorescence of my own forms.

Rather it is indirectly that I appear to the other such as I am in the faithfulness to myself – by transfiguring my appearing thanks to an interiority that remains invisible. It is impossible in a way to describe who I am, who the other is – an energy makes it so that a subject, still living, is ungraspable and, moreover, changes all the time. If it is possible to contemplate a subject, it is not possible to represent (to oneself) who this subject is – the subject has already escaped from this fixed form, from this sort of naming of what it is. Unless the subject accepts being taken, imprisoned, annihilated there. It is what is done by whoever merges into a mask, an appearance behind which one hides, in order to eventually seduce. It is also what, in a different mode, whoever repeats an already existing saying does. One submits body and spirit to already pronounced words which paralyze life, breath, energy, and prevent a living communication with the other.

To be sure language stays in us as we dwell in it. We can believe that it is our source, and that we cannot go out of its horizon. But this is not exactly the case. We live before speaking and our own origin is on this side of an already existing language. Saying ourselves cannot happen without transgressing the already learned forms. Our existence, our *hyle* – body and soul – are irreducible to the making of a technique whatever it may be, including a technique of language and, even more, irreducible to the effects that this *techné* has already produced starting from another life, from another *hyle*, than our own.

Being in Relation With the Other

Man as humanity comes to presence through his capacity for entering into relation. It is neither the definition of a being as such nor its link with the whole of being carried out in co-propriation with one unique and same subject that testifies to the Being of man. Except as a memorial of what he can make, understood as fashioning outside of himself while blindly projecting himself into it. Human being is then always already in the past, a past which prevents it from attaining the effective becoming of its real Being. Trapped in productions of an already bygone History, human being no longer works toward the construction of a History more appropriate to its Being.

This more enlightened construction requires that the subject who has elaborated History question himself about the manner in which he has done this, and understand this "how" as a manner of being which is proper to him but does not exhaust what he can be. To continue the human becoming of what he is, the subject has to introduce into his own subjectivity a dialectical movement that examines it and sets it in motion and in transformation starting from objective productions considered as an occasion of revelation of a Being partially blind to what it is. The becoming conscious of what he has made gives rise to a turning back of the subject to himself, in himself with himself (as that same that he is), a turning back from which he can start off again more conscious toward the work of the becoming of his Being. Instead of remaining imprisoned in his past works, he makes them the occasion for an unveiling of what he partially is, reopening then a future for the subject who has to construct History.

This return to oneself of the subject has been evaded because of a projection into a supposedly objective making. To come back to oneself, after such a movement, does not grant to the subject a simple unity. This gesture enlightens him about what he is and allows stepping back into self as far as what determines most irreducibly his proper mode of being. It thus serves as a way for a becoming conscious in the service of Being – in its pre-given, basic beingness, and its capacities for becoming. Recognizing our projections permits both being informed about what we are and elaborating a future making with more clear-sightedness. Advancing toward what is most veiled in oneself, the subject receives some enlightenment for a more conscious construction of his becoming.

This relation to Being returns to the objectivity of the subjective in order to inscribe in its becoming a more differentiated objective, instead of remaining a blind projection of an unrecognized subjective.

This gesture is crucial in order for the becoming to be fulfilled appropriately. It is all the more indispensable if human becoming is considered as a relation-with: with oneself, with the world, with the other.

The relation with oneself and with the world has already been evoked in its dimension as a more conscious becoming and as a means of constructing a more appropriate work. As for the relation with the other, it can only exist if each one has the capacity to remain in oneself and to be conscious of what is proper to oneself. Not as a claim to a truth and a work of universal value but as a differentiated and limited world that wants to be recognized, as is recognized the world of the other in the limits of its differentiation, of its difference.

The relation with the other cannot exist without this prior gesture of reciprocal recognition. A gesture that cannot be simply formal but will relate to a real content corresponding to the Being of the other, and moreover of oneself. This real content must be recognized subjectively as must be proposed to the other a differentiated world with which to enter into relation.

This world of one's own will not however be imposed upon the other. An availability prepares a free space for a common mediation, or rather for the search for possible mediations for the two. This space is not emptiness but a silence deliberately safeguarded for the task that the relation with the other represents. Not starting from nothing but from what each already is, provided that neither be considered as the totality of the real. And that each be disposed to dialogue with a real which is not one's own but with which one has to enter into relation as human.

The identity of man does not only presuppose a more or less veiled relation of the same with itself, as the first philosophers of the Western world teach us. It implies the relation of the same with the other.

Human identity, in fact, is doubly altered, expropriated from a same closed upon its unity. It is so because of the work in which the subject projects himself, expatriates himself. Going to a foreign land is not necessary in order to expropriate oneself from a familiar same and uncover in this way what most radically is proper to self. This process can take place through an exile of self that a making outside oneself partially represents, provided that it is accompanied by a return to oneself.

Self-identity is also expropriated in the relation with the other. But such an expropriation is required by human identity and it is, in part, without return to the same.

In the Western conception of identity as unity closed upon what is one's own, this relational dimension of the human is forgotten. As is forgotten the fact that the human is not one but two. The act of entering into relation is conceived as a relation to oneself and not as a relation to the other.

The predominant mediation in the perspective of Western identity emerges from the relation of the same with itself. Being is then understood as Being of the being of only one subject, historically masculine, still forgetful of the fact that the human as such is characterized by a specific way of entering into relation with a human different from oneself, a specific way of transforming instinctive attraction into a desire attentive to the Being of the other.

The masculine subject has in fact been more concerned with the Being of the things of the world, of his world, than with the Being of another subject. And such a gesture is not only unfaithfulness to the other, it is also unfaithfulness to oneself.

The closure of identity to self is then carried out starting from an identical-to-self which remains incomplete. It even neglects the most properly human dimension of identity. It overcomes the difficulty of standing alone in existence without reaching the moment of elaborating how to be in relation with another subject. More radically, it creates the way of Being starting from a making without posing the question of what human being as such is. The relation to the other within difference is then, as well, envisioned as an occasion of a making – children for example – and not as a privileged dimension of being human.

To consider this relation as a co-belonging of man and woman in the constitution of human identity requires rethinking what being-in-relation itself implies. Being-in-relation, in fact, is generally considered as a link of or between parts in the unity of a whole. But never has the whole been defined as composed solely of two entities, what is more of two subjectively different entities. To return to the source, to the groundless ground of the co-belonging of human being to itself and to its world, constrains us to question the relation which can exist between these two parts of the human as such, a relation until now unthought.

This questioning cannot be carried out starting from already existing representations. It demands another type of thinking in which our horizon and its constitution have to be examined. It is no longer simply a matter of integrating some new terms into a logic put in place for centuries. It is logic itself that has to be modified, the grammar of thinking.

Where this logic influenced the way of saying the identical and the same, it is compelled to question how it established such equations as the foundation of thinking. It has to turn back as far as the return into oneself of whoever formulated them in order to examine their validity. That requires going back beneath the very foundation that serves as a floor or as a roof for Western metaphysics. Man has not thought Being starting radically enough from what he is, projecting outside of himself strata of himself, thus making the return to self difficult. The world that he constructed exiles man from himself. Its architecture was not clearly conscious enough to make him able to return into self once the work was accomplished. Furthermore, the little of Being that the scaffolding of his thought has allowed him to perceive leads to his not wanting to touch the earth for fear of losing the patch of sky already glimpsed.

Thus man always wanders further away from himself toward some remote universal, forgetting that in which he belongs to the most near, forgetting that this most near is in himself or beside him, mingled with what he is. What permits him to live, he neglects. What would allow him to be faithful to Being, by freeing him from metaphysical determinations that veil the truth from him, he does not take into account. More and more chained by a priori constructions that conceal from him a possible perception of himself, of his environment. Where the forest provided him with breath and matter in order to construct a world in which to project himself, he finds a technically fabricated universe which captures his life so that he keeps very little energy, even for his use. He blindly confronts or submits to an effect of his language that he had not foreseen, that he does not understand, and that intervenes in communicating with the other to the point that this becomes difficult, even if he would want to devote himself to it.

How to approach the other if the return to oneself and to the near is henceforth impossible? If it is through ready-made ideas, sentences already pronounced, dogmas of the past and, first of all, an immutable language that we speak to the other – and, moreover, to ourselves –, what about speech? Already programmed, notably by technical artifices from which we cannot free ourselves, can it still serve to connect us to that in which we belong to our

Being? Does not a constructed world prevent the return to that place of ours where life still lives, still palpitates? That place where we live in nature – even nature itself – and not only in an already constructed universe, that place where we live together with the other in a communion preceding language itself.

In this dimension of ourselves where Being still quivers, identity is never definitively constituted, nor defined beforehand. It is elaborated in relation-with, each one giving to the other and receiving from the other what is necessary for becoming. The base and the horizon of the relation to the same are from then on questioned as a stage of History which masked Being as a relation to or with the other.

Now this place is the one where life continues to be elaborated without being paralyzed in multiple deaths, which the relation to the same entails. The identity that this relation to the same provides no doubt comforts the masculine subject in his feeling of existing. But such a comfort, if it is not recognized as an assistance to be abandoned for a return to the most original of Being, prevents acceding to it and leaves man unaccomplished.

It is always to an outside-of-oneself that man first grants Being. He thus becomes the effect of what he has regarded or constructed as external to him. He constitutes himself through his productions, these not corresponding to fruits from which he could freely detach himself, his own maturity once attained.

Hegel asserts that the absolute truth is that which knows itself and not that thought by a subject who knows himself absolutely. Being is thought starting from a supposedly objective exterior to oneself, without the subject having become objective enough to himself so as to be able to distinguish what he is from what he makes. And without the interaction with the other, with others, in the work being sufficiently analyzed. It would belong to absolute knowledge to know itself and not to man to know himself in order that his knowledge be truth.

And if Hegel tries to free philosophy from the exteriority of History itself, his own philosophy still remains exteriority in relation to the man who he is. If he takes an interest in the interiority of the absolute idea, the philosopher neglects on the other hand his own interiority. Which already made the servant-girls laugh several centuries before our era, finding it strange to lose oneself in an idea to the point of forgetting the way taken. The merit of a thinker would not be to dedicate the whole of himself to a supposedly absolute thought without returning to himself in order to see, or rather experience, how it opens him out as man. The task would be to climb little by little the calvary of the spirit without asking this to transubstantiate, in return, the flesh that has been devoted to its service. Without caring about bending the spirit as well as the body to a dialectical process that enriches both of them for a historic becoming of man as man.

Thanks to Difference

Turning back to the unthought of human becoming is indispensable. But sometimes the task of discovering it will not be easy. Because what is inadequately thought paralyzes the spirit as well as the domain to which it has applied. And to ensure the stepping back which leads to the source of thinking is not obvious – sometimes the paths and the scaffoldings have disappeared in the production of discourse, and a void has deepened. Between the forgotten Being and the one already fixed in language, the bridges are cut. A flight forward then takes the place of a dialectical movement going from the past to the future, from the future to the past, ceaselessly widening its circle.

What produces this movement is, in part, determined by the relation maintained with the other, the others. It does not turn to the emptiness of the concept nor to the circle going from plenitude to alienation. The silence of a between-two, the listening to the other, which to be sure cuts into a plenitude founded on the same but does not signify for all that an alienation, are ways which contribute toward a dialectical process of which the movement is assured by the difference between the subjects.

Such a difference resists every thematization and a representative thinking can only misjudge it, forget it. But it is this difference that ensures the becoming of a dialectic of two subjects recognized in their alterity. The movement there will no longer be circular but elliptical, given the duality of focuses and sources of impulse, of resistance, of withdrawal, of restraint. Perfection will not correspond to a movement internal to the circle of Being, as one and unique, but to a movement between two different Beings interweaving attention to the other and to his, or her, contribution and fidelity to self, including in order to secure a possible reference to this other.

In such a movement, mastery of the whole eludes each one. Becoming comprises ellipses and eclipses. Invisibility and silence take part in becoming. This becoming moreover appeals to other senses more than a speculative dialectic does. The energy that animates the process does not separate off from the body that it transforms and transfigures as a thinking is elaborated that recognizes it as the source and dwelling of Being, including what that involves of the link – past, future, and present – with the other, with the others.

This other, and the relation with them that corresponds to a part of me, can never be definitively subjected to negativity. It is rather a pretension to an Absolute founded upon my own identity that must accept the negative as marking an unsurpassable limit with regard to the existence of the other in their difference.

If the negative in speculative dialectic had for its function to reduce difference by integrating it into a more accomplished level of the Absolute, here it has the role of safeguarding difference. What is scarcely perceived of difference is then used for its persistence, not for its nullification. There will no longer be thinking or Idea capable of overcoming difference. This claim appears from now on as naïve and unfaithful with regard to Being as human. A culture of difference itself, on the other hand, is indeed on the way to a new accomplishment, both of the subjective and of the objective. There will exist no absolute Idea of such a movement which can be extrapolated from the subjects that animate it. It is its nature – if this word can still be used – to remain without end, even if moments of repose are necessary for it.

To ask God himself to guarantee this absolute place of repose and of movement perhaps represents – particularly on the part of Hegel – a form of indiscretion toward divine knowledge. Wanting the becoming of our Being to rest, first, upon a theology, would this not correspond to setting God under our feet rather than to giving him a chance to manifest himself above our heads?

Strangely, man himself has not been considered

as the productive ground of Being. The origin has rather been attributed to what appears as already produced by him. Projecting toward the past as well as toward the future that which results from an unaccomplished status of the Being which belongs to him, man finds himself encircled in a blindness that he confuses with the truth.

He also considers as the whole that which corresponds to the partiality in which he stands, and which he projects upon the whole. He fails to understand that, in order to experience the whole of what he is, he has to turn back to the place where his Being is determined as relational. Not to say that the status of this relational being was already constituted through and through. There, as for History, it will be suitable to unravel the ties woven in the process of an individual becoming in order to create others that are more crucial for human being.

So, if dependence on parents, and more generally on the adult world, is necessary for a child, it is not there that the relational world most proper to humanity is elaborated. It is after having already won autonomy that the child can discover how it belongs to a human being to enter into relation with the other. And such an unveiling is linked to what is continually forgotten: difference itself. Freed from relations of dependence imposed by its prematureness, the human can then come back to what it is most originally: not one but two. Two who are neither halves nor complementary nor opposed but who, while each one has a proper human identity to accomplish, can realize this task only by maintaining between them a relation with respect for their difference(s).

We thus have to take as the stakes of subjective becoming that which is generally forgotten: difference itself, which moreover is what, most radically, provides the relation between being and Being. It is starting from the consideration, and in some way the rectification, of a redoubled forgetting of difference that thinking must get back underway. But the representation of what is to be accomplished will from then on be lacking. If its being on the way follows an intention, this intention escapes all preestablished representation, all already conceptualized knowledge.

In other words, the step to carry out toward the becoming of the human no longer obeys a science subjected to a traditional metaphysical representation.

This step can be taken in the respect for our tradition if this tradition is recognized as the still incomplete debate that a single subject has held with himself. God, Truth, Being..., such as they have been (re)presented to us, enter into this debate. The capital letter with which they are endowed so as to designate an absolute reality is to be interpreted as a need for a transcendence in order to close off a world of one's own. In this capital letter, a right to an immunity that escapes from every dispute, even from every question, is attested to.

The circle loops back to infinity without anyone being able to step back behind its circumference in order to question its what, why, how. Whoever would try to make such a gesture would immediately be called naïve and incompetent, in other words would immediately be attributed with the logical fault that this fabricated transcendence supports because of the necessities of a single subject. Such a person would be excluded from a scientific community blind to its own beliefs, to its own bids for power. The scientific subject would thus be in contradiction with himself – claiming to draw his authority from the capacity to rationally manage the whole, he would exclude from this whole whoever would propose to enter into dialogue starting from another logic. The question of knowing whether living beings exist on other planets is acceptable to traditional science. What the scientist cannot tolerate, without changing logic, is that a living subject near to him, on the same earth, sometimes in the same house, claims to enter into a rational debate starting from a logic that is not his own. That constrains him, in fact, to change the connection between Being and being which he considered as grounded, in other words to be exposed both as subject and as guarantor of the constitution and the horizon of a world.

Such a gesture however is crucial in order to resume and continue the path of human becoming.

The ultimate reality from which the path of this becoming could start off again will no longer rest on a ground *causa sui*, in any case in the sense of a God who would alone be capable of giving an account of self. It is rather from the human and from what the human most irreducibly is that it is a question of starting off again. From the human as it objectively is before it starts to construct a language and a thinking which help to distance it from its beginning, from its prematureness without thinking it in the totality of its being.

The human in what it is objectively ever since its beginning is two, two who are different. Each part of what constitutes the unity of the human species corresponds to a proper being and a proper Being, to an identity of one's own. In order to carry out the destiny of humanity, the man-human and the woman-human each have to fulfill what they are and at the same time realize the unity that they constitute.

The unity that they form, from the beginning, as human species is of course only a first reality from which to initiate human becoming. What the ultimate unity will be, we cannot anticipate: it will depend upon the cultivation of one's Being by each one and upon the cultivation of the relation between the two. This end cannot be dependent upon only one being and it escapes representation. To defer the becoming of the dual unity of the human species to only one being or Being corresponds to a denial of the difference which constitutes this unity. From then on, difference such as it will arise again later between being and Being will already be a difference that masks the first difference, that starting from which the path of human becoming can be thought and carried out.

The difference between man and woman already exists, and it cannot be compared to a creation of our understanding. We have to take care about thinking it and cultivating it, to be sure, but starting from what exists.

The basic equation of our thought can, from then on, no longer be A = A but rather A + B = One. I could have written A + non-A = the whole, but it would then seem that the feminine is equivalent to the non-masculine or vice versa. Now the masculine and the feminine are in no case the inverse or the opposite of each other. They are different. This difference that holds between them is perhaps the most unthinkable of differences – difference itself.

In fact, such a difference cannot take place inside a whole already constituted by thought. It surely has rather as effect delimiting this whole as a part of what is to be thought. It is thus unthinkable, except in the question that the whole poses about the well-foundedness of its constitution. It is sensed only in that questioning and in the listening that it opens toward the speaking of another subject, after a negativation of the whole of merely one subject as being the whole.

Difference as such here cannot become visible for the spirit except in its initial objectivity and in certain of its effects. But these effects have been misjudged or interpreted in the horizon of thinking of only one subject, which amounts to denying their irreducible difference by reducing them to a comparative evaluation in a logic of the same.

Thus the two beings and Beings of the human species have become the two poles of a single human being who, in fact, does not exist. Invented by a masculine thinking and according to its necessities, this more or less ghostly being presents rather the characteristics of a masculine subject, but with additions and subtractions.

The two poles of the human are from then on evaluated according to a rather masculine model without for all that giving an account of all the truth of man himself.

It does not suffice therefore to move back behind the closure of this world in order to find again the whole truth. This gesture permits losing one's fondness for the illusion of being in the truth but it is not yet made with regard to the difference between the two human beings or Beings – where there is not even an emptiness opened by our thinking but only the air that separates, or should separate, two autonomous living beings. To be sure, we also find there the palpitation born from attraction that the difference between generates, like a field of forces that we have to rediscover as a reality to be thought, even before representations paralyze, and perhaps falsify, this energy as a given of the real.

What remains unthought, masked behind an immemorial forgetting is, as usual, the most simple at the level of the real but the most difficult to think in a logical economy – a difference between two terms autonomous to each other which, at the first and last level, constitute a unity.

The Trilogy of the Real

The exclusion of such a difference from thinking ends in making the two parts between which it exists and the relation between them fall again into a simple naturalness. To be man or to be woman would represent a natural identity to overcome culturally, while fulfilling the task linked to what is called a "biological destiny": reproduction.

From then on, this dimension of identity is not cultivated as human. Given the characteristics of reproduction, it is possible to say that identity then remains tied to an animality that prevents it from accomplishing a subjective becoming. What the human has at the beginning and what it has at the end are not put into relation, and that leaves in abeyance what or who it really is.

Likewise, the relation between the world and the things which make it up does not get to the bottom of the reality of their being-with. It does not sufficiently take into account the manner in which this between-two is established. If it is determined according to the particularities of a non-accomplished subject and in accordance with the necessities of only one of the two subjects forming humanity, it is not possible to say that it corresponds to a link between the first and the supreme real. It only expresses a moment of the becoming of such a link, a moment perverted on two accounts. It is perverted because it is fabricated by only one subject without letting be the real as real, particularly in its being at the disposal of the necessities of another subject. The subject who has built the world can only let be the real as such if he has himself reached the ground of his own Being. And he can leave the real at the disposal of a second subject solely insofar as he recognizes that the human species is made up of two different beings and Beings which each enter into relation with the real in a specific way.

Not accepting and respecting this permanent duality between the two human subjects, the feminine one and the masculine one, amounts to preventing one of the two – historically the feminine – from attaining its own Being, and thus from taking charge of the becoming of what it already is and of the world to which it belongs, including as made up of other humans, similar or different.

But it also means not working toward the becoming of human being as relation-to-the-other, in particular to the other as a different part of the species. The return of the masculine subject to himself as well as the constitution of the world realized by him are from then on perverted – they do not get to the bottom of the reality of the real and carry out a becoming of oneself and of the world upon incomplete and unreal bases.

What appears as the ground of Being and being, and as the between-two which joins them together, is thus fictitious. One could say partially fictitious, but to speak of truth, or Truth, as partially fictitious raises complex logical problems, even if it is important to take into consideration the part of the true that played a part in its constitution. In order to succeed in this, truth must find again the relation to an initial real that it has neglected, renouncing being calibrated to the last and supreme real that it imagined starting from a partial reality.

It appears then that the real exists as at least three: a real corresponding to the masculine subject, a real corresponding to the feminine subject, and a real corresponding to their relation. These three reals thus each correspond to a world but these three worlds are in interaction. They never appear as proper in the sense of independent of each other. And when they claim to do this, they neglect one of the three reals, which distorts the whole.

The constitution of each world, like the relation that the three maintain, cannot be founded exclusively upon a relation to the same, to a single Same, to which each part should become appropriate. That would destroy the real that they are and that they present in the world, as well as the relation between the different worlds. And no mirror can give an account of this trilogy that remains unrepresentable. It is a work of putting into relation – with oneself, with the world, with the other in the respect of their difference, and also with a common universe – that manifests this real and that elaborates it. The parts which will safeguard the development and the organization of such a work are other than those to which we are accustomed in the exercise of thinking. They call for a conversion of the way of thinking.

Memory is certainly more important here than the stockpiling of representations. Faithfulness to the real is more critical than its definitive denomination. Welcoming the new which comes from the other must replace enclosure in knowledge already acquired, learned, historically transmitted. That is to say that none of the three worlds could ever close up in a self-satisfying and sealed circle with respect to the arrival of a future foreign to the past. That is also to say that what constitutes a world and the relation between worlds cannot be univocally inspired by already determined truths, that no third party can, from an outside, govern the organization, impose its law.

Starting from the real that one is, from the real of which one perceives the existence through the relation with the other, each part of the relation, each subject, has to continue the constitution and gathering of the real present in the world.

But this does not correspond to the initial or ultimate reality perceived or constructed by a subject supposedly unique and without difference with regard to the existence and the truth of what is.

Likewise it is no longer possible in the real to oppose what grows by itself to what is made by an other. Things have become more complex. It is a matter, in fact, of being faithful to what is by nature – including in the subject as such – but of participating in its growth while respecting a proper becoming, proper to oneself and proper to the other. Continually, a natural growth and a cultural becoming determined by oneself and by the other interact in this way. The opposition between original nature and final production no longer exists. Or, to say it in Aristotelian terms, between material cause and efficient cause applied to the material cause. Regarding the final cause, it must be modalized differently.

The relation to the other cannot be structured by the utilization of means with an end in mind. The material real, that the other in part represents, cannot be submitted to the aim that I give myself in the relation to him, or to her. Alas! it still generally happens this way, whether it is a question of reducing the other to a place of reproduction, to an instrument of pleasure or of work in the strict sense, or of submitting the other's becoming to the order of the same defined by only one subject.

Each subject must come to a standstill before the other, respect the irreducible alterity of the other. The help that each provides to the other's growth must be appropriate to each one's initial real and becoming, as far as each is faithful to such a real.

Whoever helps has to remain faithful to their own real. In this way the assistance provided can be efficacious as it maintains the distance and the difference between the two subjects.

Efficiency thus no longer corresponds to the application of an intention of one's own to the real that the other presents, but to listening to the other and to the sending back of the subject to what they are. In the duty to be and to become oneself, a relational dimension intervenes that the other must respect and cultivate. It is important to present oneself to the other as different in order for this relational present effectuation and becoming to be practicable.

If some technique takes part in the relation between subjects, it is thus of a quite different sort than that to which we are accustomed. It is no longer a question of a subject submitting a real to his own ends, nor even of unveiling its truth by his own means. Turning back to a silent real in order to let the other appear and express their self could instead represent a first manner of corresponding to this real in an appropriate way.

But can this way still be designated as a technique? Unless we recognize that technique itself can take negative paths: withdrawals, silences, questionings, etc. which do not amount to what we consider as a making.

This has appeared to us, in fact, as an operation exterior to the subject, through which the subject transforms a matter thanks to an instrument with an end in view. Making has seldom been considered as a work carried out inside subjectivity itself starting from and upon what the subject already is and with a becoming in mind. Such a work of interiority remains almost unknown to us. Perhaps because the relation with the other has not been sufficiently recognized as a decisive part of subjectivity. And because philosophy, as an undertaking of the Western masculine subject, has dedicated itself to transforming a real exterior to the subject in order to appropriate it.

No doubt this operation has effects upon the subject. It encloses him, in particular in his own productions. Nothing there that leads the subject to the blossoming of what he is as relation with the other. To be sure he will be able to offer to the other something of the transformation carried out upon matter through his technique. That does not amount to becoming adapted to welcoming the speech of the other in oneself and to accepting that this speech questions us, expels us from a house of language built from and with a view to the same. Nor to giving the other what is appropriate to their own Being and becoming.

In a sense, the relation with the other leads to

renouncing what we usually consider as a finality. It constrains us to keep finality in suspense, so as to let the other be, to let the other come to encounter us without subjecting this other to our world. The finality of the one is not necessarily that of the other. In the other a stranger, a different culture approaches us that we cannot reduce to ourselves, to our imperatives.

Neither can we steal the other's energy, appropriate it in order to accumulate resources or to work on other unfoldings of our Being. The other is not at our disposal unless we fail in our human identity, become ourselves machines in the service of technique. The other cannot serve as a resource for our project, our action. In the constitution of a human horizon, the other must remain an other, someone different with whom to learn how to live together and to dialogue.

From then on, the other is what marks the limit of the use and influence of technology, and of the power of the technologist. Not in the manner of a controversy for which a solution or common resolution will be sought and finally found. Because such an appeasement risks corresponding to the reduction into a new same of what is most irreducible in human identity: the relation in duality.

The solution of a possible coexistence for the two

subjects who make up the human species is, at each moment, to be negotiated starting from the different manner in which they live the relation to oneself, to the other, to the world. It neither is nor can be unique, identical, same. Nor appear as a simple controversy. The disagreement that the one must resolve is not the same as that to be resolved by the other. Being-with is to be found rather in the relinquishing of a common solution or truth, which does not mean settling into an in-finite controversy. Recognizing difference requires renouncing even this in order to accede to a less immediate relational culture, one more conscious of the insurmountable limits of each subjectivity, of the irreducibility to the one, to the same. A gesture which demands a maturity capable of being on the way alone.

Making/Letting Be

This presupposes that we renounce imperatives born from the subjection of the one to the other: a making of beauty or a making of erection, for example. That we carry out a return to an accomplishment which more fully allows an initial real to blossom without substituting a product of technique for it. Submitting raw material to a making often amounts to causing it to vanish in an end imposed from outside rather than letting its properties appear. This gesture is all the more to be avoided if the real corresponds to a human being which, in itself, gathers together matter, a proper life, and consciousness. To subject such a real to a technique that transforms it with a view to a finality other than its own becoming is doubly inhuman, reducing the human itself, in oneself and in the other, to a being-at-the-disposal without faithfulness to resources of its own.

These resources are perhaps un-covered last, like an original daybreak always concealed and forgotten insofar as it is confused with the beginning of Being itself. Thus what is properly human is not easily unveiled and it is not some science which will be able to give an account of it starting from a calculation external to it. The hypotheses and operations of a science already act upon a matter lacking the consciousness that gathers it together and animates it. Likewise, to go search in other species or kingdoms for the secret capable of aiding in the unveiling of the human as such amounts to preventing this human from manifesting itself. Because its taking-place obeys only the imperatives of humanity. Neither the behavior of the amoeba nor that of the rat will lead the way toward the blossoming of the subject as such. Certain dimensions critical for such a blossoming are lacking in them. And only through assuming the whole of what it is, and through respecting its organization in what is proper to it, can the human go on the way toward an ultimate Being unveiling an initial being.

Historically, man has not ceased to project himself forward without questioning what animates him. Leaving his first and final cause to beings anterior or posterior to the living being that he is, he did not place his cause in himself. This gesture would have induced him to care more about his own becoming, particularly in its dimension of coexistence with living beings, the same and other than himself but belonging to the same species.

From these other living beings, he also draws his source – of Being, of becoming. Besides the fact of being engendered by one of them, strictly speaking by two, he receives from them assistance, energy, impulse. His own movement is not determined by him alone, whether it is a matter of reaching an already represented aim or of a going-toward without any end determined beforehand.

What is truly proper to a subject is both much and very little. To cultivate one's singularity requires an attention to each moment in order to distinguish what belongs to one's birth, growth, consciousness, and what belongs to the world or to the age in which the subject lives. The most near is often assimilated to one's own, not distinguished from oneself. And to merge into a universal described as 'human' is often preferred to stopping to analyze the difference between oneself and the other. The tendency is to adapt oneself to or appropriate the most distant as little differentiated rather than to consider who one is and who the other is in the relation with those, men or women, around one. It will be necessary that the foreigner come into one's own country or that the subject go to foreign lands for a question to arise about the diversities that compose the human species. But often these will be reduced to secondary elements or limited to a simple genetic inheritance and not envisioned in their subjective differences. To restore some contrast in this disquieting flood of the universal, this new deluge that threatens humanity as such, man confronts from now on the remote verticality of other planets endowed with hypothetical inhabitants, without understanding that he could find a salvation in what distinguishes him from what is most near.

Such a questioning is the one that can today awaken consciousness, give rise to another way of thinking, return to the human real as it is originally so as to lead it to a blossoming without sacrificing its singularity.

Can this gesture take place outside an encounter with another consciousness? Without attention to another world here beside me and, moreover, in part already in me? From which I am separable only through recognizing it as different. Fecund thanks to its irreducible light, its unsubstitutable speaking but also the limit that it imposes on an expansion in which my energy gets lost, and the meaning that I can give to it. Thanks to the obligation to return to me, in me, where the initial real of which I have to care for the becoming can be found.

This real, in myself as in the other, contains in itself the possibility of blossoming. Its unfolding, its flowering do not depend upon the making of someone other. In this sense, the human remains tied to nature. And when it takes root in History without fidelity to nature, it alienates there its particularity and the task of producing it as such, among other things for the construction of a present and future History. The human also loses in this the occasion to elaborate in the present its relation with the other. And what it considers as the most human of its work then becomes non-human. Or, at least, that which continually puts off the unveiling and the accomplishment of what the human as such is. Which makes the human itself hybrid: what it produces arising from it, at least in part, without relating to or unfolding the ground of what it is. The one who should gather together and organize the whole, then fragments into this or that part, for lack of starting from and respecting in its work the real that it is, at least originally.

In this way, man loses the intuition of what he is, and lets himself be governed by that which distances him more and more from himself. Even what are called the human sciences approach this real from the outside, with the aid of calculations and techniques that make the "soul" dissolve before even reaching the question of what constitutes the Being of man in his ground, his existence, his particularity with respect to other kingdoms. Deprived of soul, a coherence from then on will be provided for him thanks to a totality foreign to what animates his life and his becoming: an essence, or a unique divine being of which the properties are immutable. Unities defined through abstraction at a moment of the human journey and which prevent this journey from unfolding between its first and last terms.

And to speak of destiny – as Heidegger often does –, is this not still to refer to something external to man? Would it not be more fitting to speak of strata of Being which are progressively fulfilled in History? The accomplishment of History taking place when the most original of the real discovers how to blossom all the way to the ultimate level of the cultural. In order to advance toward this stage, the question of man as being capable of entering into relation with the other, in the respect for difference(s) between subjects, is critical. It is still to be considered and implemented, buried in an initial real that constitutes the human as such.

The undertaking that it demands is different from the one generally at work in Western metaphysics. To accept not to make, in favor of a letting be, is a gesture required for turning back to the ground of oneself and for recognizing the other as other. Then the reason for the importance of making for man can be unveiled, for the necessity to produce outside himself by imposing his intention upon a matter still apparently without form. And the most crucial question appears not only as: why has man produced this or that thing in some epoch of History, but: why has man, throughout History, privileged making? And how to interpret the relations between making and being, particularly with the meaning of letting be? Does not their traditional opposition mask an inappropriate articulation between nature and culture that prevents man from knowing himself in his truth?

Does arriving at this ultimate unveiling really put man in danger? Perhaps. Unless he discovers that humanity is two, and that he is from now on faced with a new task, without doubt the most crucial for his becoming. While the Being of man was revealed through a producing exterior to himself, through things of his world, here he is confronted with a doing without any exterior object. The way of thinking then remains inside oneself and results from a dialogue with another subject, irreducible both to oneself and to an object. One might as well say foreign to the world which was, up until now, that of man.

If man thus discovers himself as the origin of all making, he does not have to be simply delighted about it. He must regard the reality of this dominance as an outcome of the forgetting of what he most fundamentally is as human: a being in relation with the other, and as an outcome of the lack of comprehension of his most human task: to lead the relation with the other from nature to culture without abolishing the duality of subjectivities.

Discovering that he is lord of the earth, man then discovers that he is not the only subject who inhabits it, and that the cultivation of the real must from now on be shared. To be sure such a truth entails some dangers but not that of an almighty facing an abyss. And the difficulties that are announced also represent a solution inasmuch as they bring to the masculine subject the means of finding a limit elsewhere than in the saturation of an epoch of History through his own producing.

This salvation also occurs because man is then sent back to a truth not exclusively dependent upon a making external to him. The return to himself that man must carry out in order to find again his initial real also brings him back to a form of production of the true that he had forgotten: one which respects, in appearing, the coming into the present and the letting be, including of himself.

In the new temporality of a becoming, which then emerges, the opposition between an unfolding of truth tied to nature and an unveiling of a truth in which nature is subjected to a making of man is overcome. The blossoming of man requires, in fact, a making and a letting be. In the return or the turning back toward man that the age of technique as such leads to, technique thus finds its limit and its safeguard – both in the unveiling of the importance of a letting nature be, including for and in culture, and in the fact that nature and its cultivation appear then as irreducibly dual and implying a relation between the two unities or worlds which make them up.

In this way a temporality, which the sovereignty of technology endangers, can be reconstituted. The subject risks, in fact, being fragmented there in his products and without a possible return to himself given the type of mediations playing a part in production. Moreover, the domination exercised by technique or technology itself destroys temporality because it is no longer structured by a subject.

To come back to the place always to be re-articulated between nature and culture, between letting be and constructing, necessitates implementing a temporality until now unknown. Taking into consideration and practicing the relation with the other in the respect of difference(s) also and at the same time compels it.

There, in fact, a duration is constituted of which human consciousness is the artisan, taking charge of the cultivation of the human real and its blossoming. Such a duration returns at each moment to its source, to the place of an encounter that always in part is new. It does not directly extend to the dimension of an epoch of History for example, putting between the other and oneself all the constructedness of this. It is in the silence of a not-yet-come-to-pass that it is elaborated, weaving in two voices past, present, and future. In every moment, each lays oneself open to the other, running the risk of losing one's way in a lack of recognition. Each then turns back in oneself in order to take up again a faithfulness to self and a growth in accordance with an initial real. Between this truth of oneself and that heard from the other, a temporality is created which is composed by two, never subjecting one to the other, never using one for the production of the other. The withdrawal of each in oneself, like the memory that each keeps of the speaking of the other, conjoins two ways of safeguarding and cultivating the truth. These ways must not become confused on pain of overshadowing what duality provides for human becoming. Each one even has to preserve in oneself the other as other, to protect the other from the loss of self in a real or a same not appropriate to what they really are. But each one also has to safeguard the other from shining in such a way that they could no longer assure the necessary return in themselves that their blossoming and the relation with an other demands. Even for their own benefit, neither of the two can push the other to ecstasy in an appearing – of oneself, or of a world – in which the real at one's disposal is exhausted. And if each human is called to become a work of art, it is in a way in accordance with its being and not in the manner of an object produced by some other for their own enjoyment.

Engendered Not Created by One Another

The work of art that a human is invited to carry out is first the blossoming of self in its own singularity. Which presupposes a still unknown cultivation of space and time.

Thus it is not by overcoming distances that the

human will find proximity to self, to the other, nor even to the world. It is rather in the capacity to stay in oneself, to exist in one's autonomy, distinct from what surrounds one. It is also in the ability to proceed from oneself while recognizing the part of the other in this provenance.

The appropriate name for such a participation of the other in the provenance of self is perhaps engendering. The human is not made by the other in the manner of a thing, but proceeds from the other as engendered by the other, at the natural and spiritual level.

Whether in his body or in his 'soul,' also called spirit, a man thus originates in an other from whom he has to differ, as mother, and with whom, as woman, he has to find alliance. Being engendered for him does not take place once and for all: the human cannot detach itself from her from whom it is born, like a thing with regard to whoever fabricated it. For the human it is not the same, and the interiority which takes place in oneself through the conquest of one's autonomy does not correspond to a container available for receiving all that which will be poured into it. At least it should not be so, resulting from the elaboration of a separation from an other which should modify and not abolish the relation to the one who has engendered.

The soul should not be an empty space situated in man – as it is in a vase – for receiving what would come to fill it from an outside. At least not simply. Because the soul is already received, or should already be received, from she who engenders, and from the transformation into culture of the relation with her. Thus, the space of the soul is already inhabited and does not amount to emptiness, to nothing. Nevertheless that in which the soul is inhabited must not prevent the welcoming of the other, particularly the other as different – from oneself, from she who engenders –, an other thanks to whom being engendered will be carried out with the conscious consent and participation of those who agree in this way to continue to proceed so as to let blossom more fully who they are.

The generation and the becoming of the subject as engendered will thus continue. This is no longer only passive, but a letting-grow that is conscious and in which the subject participates. The subject lets itself be engendered while helping the process of generation. Such a becoming is then corporeal and spiritual, material and conscious, which permits both recognition and reciprocity between the engendered and the engendering. An act which was, originally, apparently univocal, becomes biunivocal. The mother seems to unilaterally engender the child, but, as adults, man and woman have the responsibility of continuing to engender themselves reciprocally. This is possible thanks to their difference(s), which cannot be evaluated in comparative, quantitative terms, but in properties able to produce different effects which allow them to fecundate one another.

Such an engendering is not simply physical, even if it is not totally foreign to the material constitution of each one. But reciprocity in the respect for differences supposes that each one accepts this constitution, at physical and psychic levels, and enters into fruitful relation with the other. That implies blossoming in what is proper to oneself and contributing toward the blossoming of the other in what is proper to him, or her. Such a work is doubly creative of the spiritual, of soul. To blossom presupposes recognizing who has engendered you and remaining grateful toward her. Thus no question of repudiating this beginning or of using it for a culture founded upon oblivion. In oneself, a space must be safeguarded which remembers, acknowledges, gives thanks, and reciprocates as much as it is possible in a genealogical relation foreign to simple reciprocity.

In this way a place opens in which the growth of the subject is not limited to the physical without being for all that totally foreign to it. In this place, thoughts and intentions relative to the other exist, as well as a receptiveness. Such a relation is accompanied by values related to it, more hierarchical than those which grow in the horizontal relation between woman and man.

There, no more abyss from below or from on high, no more regression toward the mystery of the origin or elevation toward the ultimate perfection, barring repetition. The task is to prepare a path to the other as other, by transforming the attraction for him, or her, into matter to work out in a human relation. Instinctive attraction is retained, kept, but, thanks to the renunciation of being exercised immediately, changes with a view to a manifestation capable of being appropriate to the one who desires and the one who is desired.

The feast of love then can be celebrated, gathering together the mortal and the divine, the earthly and the celestial in an encounter where giving and receiving are exchanged in the elation of the present. This present provides the bridge between past and future insofar as it retains the perceived attraction in order to make it a gift to the other, while adapting this giving to the memory of the other, and insofar as the present consents to receive what the other will offer and what will result as blessings from the feast celebrated together. Then the present is constructed by the two, and perhaps it cannot be otherwise, the present always occurring in an encounter-between – as between mortals and divinities, earth and sky.

The present is what assembles and gathers together. Between past and future, a space free but laid out by the soul, the spirit, or the heart must be safeguarded where the advent of the encounter can take place. This vacant reserve is the preliminary offering made by each one in the invitation to meet. Body and soul, space and time enter into it. As a suspension of the becoming of self and one's own world in order to make oneself available for what such a growth has to construct with the other, without for all that renouncing oneself.

Little by little the work of becoming oneself then combines continuously with that of the other in an interweaving of spaces and times where visible and invisible alternate. The opposition between the light of the sun and the light of reason is overcome here insofar as, in the other, both lights show through, and the eyes of the body can gaze upon the one and the other without having to sacrifice this sight for more or less faithful reflections of ideas reproduced in the shadow of an obscure chamber named spirit, or even for reflections of which each one would passively be the medium or the mirror.

It goes otherwise. And what was designated as representations, objects, things, etc. has to be interpreted as effects of some presence in the present where the relation with the other is forgotten. These modes of presentation of the truth in fact are the offspring of an obliteration of the presence of the other in memory, in intention, in present perception. They are masks upon the present real of Being and of its becoming, and what or who produces them or makes them possible is already extrapolated from this real.

How thus to draw near to it? Certainly not by believing that one can bring together from the outside fragments of what already is, or appears as such. Because, in the gesture of putting near, something gets lost of approaching or drawing closer together: proximity. It is not deliberately and thanks to one alone that proximity can be joined. It implies letting oneself be reached by what draws near, and accepting that, in this bringing together, the proper of a world opens up for welcoming the other.

The recognition of the other as different means that approaching involves an irreducible distancing. This distancing lies, insurmountable, in the drawing near to one another, like an elusive mystery that we transgress ceaselessly in an anticipation of desire, but of which the preservation is necessary in order that desire unfold toward a blossoming which does not happen without withdrawal. Nor without accepting that, in the present, an invisible intervenes at the level of representation – of things, objects, concepts.

In order to welcome the other, it is rather to perception that it is important to return seeing, on the condition however that seeing not claim that all become visible and that it not conceal this lack of visibility through representation.

The pretension to know the other, or the will to integrate the other into one's own world, do not allow approaching him, or her. What could assist such a gesture would be rather the definition of mediations permitting each one, man or woman, to subsist, to be, and to become in their difference without for all that renouncing the relation between the two.

From the outside, man and woman cannot be approached. But the existence of mediations proper to each favors a coexistence in difference where drawing near to one another in the preservation of distance becomes possible.

When the world is closed by what is proper to only one, it assembles within an encircling of the horizon in which each one belongs to the whole and the whole to each one. Thus, no open space between the one and the other, between each one and the whole that permits safeguarding difference and its productive play. Each one and the whole are already appropriated to a same and the link between them in fact transpropriates – a second time – the whole and each one to this same. Instead of remaining faithful to one's first and last Being, of cultivating it in the present in relation to the other with respect for differences, in the gathering together of the whole each is expropriated ecstatically from oneself, the other, the reality of one's world in a specular reproduction supposedly common but appropriate to only one and the same culture founded notably upon the reflection, the projection, the ecstasis of oneself and one's universe in Truth or Being.

A culture founded above all upon the forgetting of difference as it distances and brings closer the two parts of humanity: man and woman. Who have nothing proper to put in common in a way, at least nothing exterior to them as subjects. What they could put in common has to be elaborated by them starting from a different energy. This energy must be cultivated in order to enter into relation with the other; it must be retained, kept, transformed, while remaining proper, in order to be shared with the other without expropriating the other or being expropriated oneself from the place where this energy is born.

Then the relation between each one, between each one and the whole does not become transpropriated in a unique reflection-place – a different, more spatial, version of the spirit of a people. It saves its memory in each one, where an alliance between earth and sky, human(s) and divinity(ies) takes place in a proper manner, an alliance that is carried out through the relation to oneself, to the other, to the world. To be sure, in our culture, something of this memory is kept, but often it has lost, at least in part, its availability because of its entrapment in already coded forms, moreover coded unilaterally.

Poetic language sometimes keeps available a part of the energy of the coming into relation, and that of thinking when it exists. The two are moreover separated much less than the Western tradition has claimed.

Rebuilding the World

The Other at the Crossroads Between Past and Future, Between Earth and Sky

It is not in a thing that we can save the memory of the world as a bringing into relation of earth and sky, mortals and gods. Unless we say that the soul, or the spirit, are similar to a thing. But they ought to carry out their becoming and not remain a simple remembering. Perhaps between man and woman they became distributed in such a way that the one acts outside himself and the other keeps inside herself. If this corresponds to a thoughtless tendency of an initial Being, the final blossoming cannot be attained through this simple complementarity.

In each one, memory must be preserved for one's own becoming and a future encounter with the other. Each one is then a receptacle which conserves in order to share, while continuing to elaborate past and future.

Even the relation is a kind of receptacle to be cared for by each one, a place where that which will allow a feast to come is remembered and retained. This space is not solely internal to each one but it does not correspond to a simply external thing, and which only one ought to fashion. This – ultimate? – undertaking of humanity is more complex and far more subtle.

Diverse realities have concealed the possibility of

such a work: the child, for example, but also the univocal conception of a human Being endowed with a vertical transcendence supposedly corresponding to it. In a transcendence of this sort, the difference that founds humanity in its initial real is forgotten, a real that we have to cultivate in the respect of a horizontal transcendence, without simply extrapolating it into a wholly Other belonging to the beyond of this world.

What seems difficult for humanity is to ensure a duration. Often it is to matter that, paradoxically, it entrusts this task: the house, the child, the woman as nature. The culture elaborated by Western man has claimed to overcome the natural universe through ideas, words, things, concepts ... which do not safeguard its memory. Forgetful of the initial being of each human, this tradition is without return to self. In order to anchor its duration, it moors itself to what still is made of matter, without remembering its own spiritual evolution, thus without a possible faithfulness to itself, except in some stages of a collective becoming.

Man has seldom taken into consideration that remembering also finds its possibility in oneself. Rather his culture appears founded upon the forgetting of oneself. Man extrapolates his self into ideas, forms, things, concepts ... in which he suspends himself in order to free himself from Being.

The same in which he dwells, moreover, does not amount, in all strictness, to the same as himself, even if it is constructed by man in a will, more or less veiled, to live with himself and in his own world.

But, wanting to build without caring about the other, man has also contributed to expropriation from himself. Particularly from a memory of himself. This seems to exist only thanks to the relation with the other in difference. Then time no longer freezes in a reflection where the self remains in suspense. It returns to itself in order to continue the becoming, of the self and of the relation with the other. Remembering needs this return which can be granted in becoming conscious that the same is inappropriate for completely giving an account of man.

In every reflection, in fact, man loses his volume and the asymmetry of the living being which constantly confronts him. In the inversion of himself that reflection presents, he renounces life without for all that reaching the Being of death. He loses as well the perspective necessary for perceiving the reality of the world, of the other. Everything becomes images, external or internal, in which the look also becomes extrapolated from itself, taken away into the spectacle,-without a possible return.

In this non-return, vision loses its ability to perceive the real, the living as a volume always unfinished, mobile, in becoming. Something of binocular vision is forgotten, and of the difference between oneself and the other. Everything becomes trapped in the same reflection without any trace of the interval that the restoration of that which separates this reflection from the real brings about. Alterity gets lost in a specular play not perceived as such. The reversal of view is then effaced, the turning around of which would restore to each their body, their two eyes, and their memory. And an articulation of time irreducible to a series of juxtapositions that come together only in the global vision of a whole participating in the same horizon. Thus without duration in a way.

The mirror suspends time in an indeterminate space. A priori or a posteriori, there is no longer space or time available for a living human who enters into such a culture. The human is left ossified in its possibility of existing. Frozen in front of what it is presumed to be and to become. The model that it obeys is no longer incarnated in this or that idol which it would have chosen, it is imposed through an idea of humanity to which it is supposed to have to conform. The modalities of the relation to oneself, to the other, to the world are prescribed by culture, and the freedom to act in a different way is minimal. Such freedom implies both leaving the construction of a tradition and entering into relation with a human belonging to the other part of humanity carrying out the same gesture.

Sages have sensed the difficulty of the task. Perhaps they did not perceive the significance of the relation with the other for its realization. In this obligation to reckon with the other as other, we find a way of going and coming from the past to the future, from the future to the past without forgetting the present. We regain a necessary mobility and evolution of time, founded upon need and desire, fidelity to oneself and fidelity to the other, remembering and planning. Memory becomes clouded by a culture extrapolated from the presence to oneself and to the other in the present. The bridge that it provides only works starting from the experience of each singularity.

The teaching of History cannot substitute for an individual memory without running the risk of subjecting such a remembering to an already existing representative model, which amounts to annihilating it as remembrance of the personal present or past. That which remained the condition and the foundation of culture is thus sent back to oblivion in favor of instructions abstracted from any subjective experience.

Such teachings then participate in the play of reflections that dominate our tradition, depriving the subject who enters into it of self, leading this subject into a world of suggestion and of fascination in which any real disappears.

Experience is no longer inscribed in the body by perception, memory. It is immediately subjected to specular and speculative standardizations.

Thus to dwell is, according to Hölderlin for example, a fundamental trait of the human condition. But being able to dwell would be tied to the act of constructing: without building, there would be no dwelling. A house, however, could be made of language and to construct could correspond to a poetic activity.

To construct only in order to construct nevertheless does not suffice for dwelling. A cultivation of the living must accompany a building of that which does not grow by itself.

For a human, the two do not seem separable. To cultivate human life in its engendering and its growth requires the elaboration of material and spiritual frameworks and constructions. These should not be opposed to the becoming of life, as they have too often been, but provide it with the help indispensable for its blossoming.

This blossoming depends upon two dimensions: vertical and horizontal. Here again, our culture has favored verticality, the relation to the Idea allegedly at the summit of approximate reproductions, the relation to the Father, to the leader, to the celestial Wholly-Other. The relation to the other, present here and now beside or in front of me on the earth, has been little cultivated as a horizontal dimension of human becoming. Now this dimension is probably even more specific to humanity than verticality, if at least it involves the respect for the other in their irreducibility, their transcendence.

In a relation to a Wholly-Other extrapolated from its world, it is still itself that the human most often seeks. It suffices to question the gods or the God with which humans have provided themselves in order to realize this. And, when sexual difference appears in the representations of these gods, it may frequently be noted that the properties of one or the other sex or gender vary according to the voice of the one who culturally speaks most loudly. Likewise, the valorization granted to one's own sex or to that of the other depends on the gender, masculine or feminine, of the subject who attributes it. The emphasis put on the ascending or descending character of genealogy undergoes the same fluctuations.

To search in the representative of an absolute difference for the image of oneself or an ideal of oneself is not the most cultivated gesture to which a human can aspire. It remains on several accounts childish, naïve, unconcerned about the relation with the other that it is incumbent upon humanity to live in a conscious and not purely instinctive manner. In such a gesture, the human also remains unable to return to self, at least to the most original of the real that constitutes it. The human then does not practice the renouncing to be the whole that opens the way to an alliance with the other. And that provides oneself and one's world with limits.

The interval deepened, without ever being filled, by the difference between oneself and the other, that should correspond to the basic gesture of a human culture. From this results the hollow space for dwelling, in oneself and outside oneself, laid out through both a cultivation of natural life and a construction of relations between humans not opposed to this natural life.

The creation and the safeguarding of such a space extends beyond the time of childhood and that of simple needs. And it does not amount to the construction of a house of wood or of stone in order to protect oneself from bad weather nor to dwelling in a house of language in order to take shelter from oneself and others. What thus is built is not only a refuge. It is also a space where the horizon of the already lived and defined reopens. A space where the bridge between past, present, and future is elaborated, as well as the passages between the other and oneself.

The difficulty in this creative faithfulness is that no external measure can assess the validity or value of what is built. At least no standard exists which could be applied from the outside in order to judge the task. It is to a more interior undertaking that the human is invited here, to a work of becoming that can be evaluated according to the blossoming of the Being of the self, of the other, of the world where they dwell.

If a recourse to the divine is then necessary, this cannot be to the detriment of the divine of the other, nor of the divine to cultivate between oneself and the other. Which implies that the celestial lies not only above our head but also between us. It rises then originally from the attraction existing between woman and man, women and men, and the cultivation of this attraction. No figuration or representation belonging to only one gender will be privileged there, and the relation to nature is never totally overcome. The sky and the earth remain linked and their separation leads to the loss of the one and of the other – as is the case moreover for the cosmic universe.

Humans do not discover the measure of their becoming only in a relation to the celestial but also in the respect of the terrestrial as such. That humans give themselves divine representations as supports of becoming, very well, but what are these worth if they do not favor natural growth, drawing upon it as well.

Macrocosm and microcosm in this way remain dialectically linked with the spiritual becoming of each one. Moreover, they are present in the relation with the other, leading to elevation toward the sky and return toward the earth, a rising of energy toward the summit of the body and a descent toward its base. The heart being the place where energy most continuously finds its impulse and its repose? The heart remaining what most constantly links sky and earth, sustaining itself on the lowest and the highest, on the real in what is most elemental and most sublime in it?

The Intimate Requires Separate Dwellings

By alternating between moving and resting, going toward the other and turning back within oneself, spiritual evolution and the irradiating of the body by a more subtle energy, a duration is woven which, certainly, differs from a linear course or a perpetual repetition or tautology. Time itself becomes, neither pure cosmic economy or biological progress nor pure human construction. The two intertwine, in each one and between one another, so as to build a possible dwelling for humans. Time itself becomes space, doubles spatiality without for all that surrounding it. Time and space remain open while continuously constituting a dwelling place in which to stay. Its measure is found in a perceiving of oneself and of the other, in a listening to oneself and to the other, and also to that third which arises and to grows from the two and which, too quickly and to its detriment, is assimilated to a child.

When this third – neither simple exterior law nor simple common production – is not misunderstood, measure cannot be reduced to a length of which we would dispose according to our will. It also takes place in a letting be and a letting come to us what reaches us through the other – already thanks to desire but also through the gift that he, or she, offers us of self, of the world, and of ourselves as welcomed and gathered by him, or her.

The measure for the human thus has to be assessed not only with respect to the distance stretching between earth and sky, and the dimensions which it confronts are more complex than a being-on or a being-under. The return to oneself, into oneself, creates in this expanse that goes from the terrestrial to the celestial inner spaces, which require being evaluated differently. To go toward the other, to welcome the other into oneself open non-vertical dimensions in the relation to the human and to the divine.

The expanse that man must measure is thus

neither linear, nor uniform, nor homogeneous. In the composition between the high and the low, the in-front and the in-back, the within and the without, the enveloping and the enveloped ... are generated spaces of which the curves, the loops can provide places in which to take shelter. Not of course in a definitive manner but the time of a pause – for repose, for thought, for inward gathering. Also for distanciation, an estrangement which will permit coming together.

Without a return into oneself, how still to approach the other? To respect the other in their mystery? As invisibility to be sure, but also as proximity with oneself which needs distance in order to touch oneself again, to find oneself again, to restore the integrity of intimacy with oneself.

Too entrusted to a certain look or a certain listening-to in the service of representation, the relation with the other has forgotten what it owes to touching – among others visual and acoustic touching. Then the approach becomes seizure, capture, comprehension, all gestures of incorporation, introjection, apprehension in which the other as such vanishes. Rather it is arranging dwelling places safeguarding the proper of each one which is imperative in order to favor proximity. And not only images or metaphors which express, while concealing, one's invisibility. But places where each one lives, separated, and where each restores the weaving of proximity with oneself. Preparing for an encounter cannot be reduced to covering the other with clothes, images, or speeches which render this other familiar to us, but requires finding gestures or words which will touch the other in his, or her, alterity.

Drawing near necessitates allying two intimacies, not submitting one to the other. Attraction is often awakened by the difference between two worlds, by the mystery that the one represents for the other. To cover the other with the figments of my imagination favors without doubt a violation or a theft of this mystery but not an approach between us. Such an approaching can exist in the respect of two familiarities which wed without canceling each other out. To include the other in my universe prevents meeting with the other, whereas safeguarding the obscurity and the silence that the other remains for me aids in discovering proximity.

Such a proximity is not similar to the one that we can experience with regard to things. The relation with things is not reciprocal as it can be with another human, and the familiarity that we share with them is often our own. That things impose on us a certain resistance does not imply that they cultivate with themselves and for themselves an intimacy of their own, like that of which a human is capable. The secret that the thing opposes to us is perhaps the one that an other has deposited in it. It is not its own secret.

The human, however, is capable of secrecy. At least as long as the human does not sacrifice itself to a calculating madness, as long as the human does not fragment what it is and that which surrounds through a submission to inappropriate measures. Human mystery must be safeguarded and cultivated thanks to a poetic way of dwelling. And the same goes for the preservation of the mystery of the other, whose attraction lives on if this other continues to surprise without being reduced to some familiar evaluation at our disposal.

Poetic dwelling, from then on, goes beyond covering or surrounding the whole with images and reflections finding their unity in some round dance. We have to discover another means of approaching. This does not cover each one and each thing with a same, with something supposedly proper to everything and everyone. Rather it advances step by step toward an un-covering, of oneself and of the other, which reopens the place where each one takes shelter to prepare the moment of an encounter. From this, each one will receive oneself and will turn back, modified, toward a dwelling that will need to transform its frame in order to secure the memory of becoming – of oneself, of the other, of the world.

The gestures and words that we have to invent will be appropriate therefore to an opening outside the horizon of the identical, of the similar, of the familiar to one alone. Going toward discovering a common same – supposing that it exists – will not favor the encounter either but will impede its coming to term.

The approach is possible only in the recognition of the irreducible difference between the one and the other. This, in fact, gives access to a path from the one to the other and to the sharing of a still free energy and space. Only in what is still independent of the influence of someone, may proximity take place as event and advent. Something comes to pass which does not belong as one's own to the one or to the other. Something arrives which did not exist and that the bringing together of two worlds produces. What in this way occurs gives itself to each one inasmuch as he, or she, wants to welcome it, and to secure its memory. Not in order to keep it as a thing but as the mysterious legacy of an encounter which it is important to remember without simply appropriating it.

The beloved is sheltered in the silence of the heart, in the mystery of thinking, in the restraint of the gesture, its inward gathering, and a self-touching guaranteeing a possible safeguarding of the other and of the world. The opening needs the possibility of returning to oneself, into oneself. Of finding again, for a moment, the repose of a dwelling. Of letting be and letting grow the fruits of the encounter in the withdrawal of a proximity with oneself. Which, in part, remains nocturnal and silent. The near requires the invisible, the relinquishing of designation by a word, letting be made or remade the integrity of the self.

In order to be able to welcome the other, a certain fullness must be restored, which escapes the control of a will. Time is indispensable for such a reconstitution which will permit the memory of oneself, of the other, of their difference and of their approach. The other cannot be kept, sheltered thanks to a simple decision. Irreducible to us, we cannot apprehend the other in order to provide a dwelling for them. This place of hospitality for the other becomes built as much as, if not more than, we build it deliberately. Made of our flesh, of our heart, and not only of words, it demands that we accept that it takes place without our unilaterally overseeing its construction. It is in secret that it unfolds without any mastery by our seeing, by our domination through language. Remaining hidden, the other can be safeguarded. And it is certainly not when unveiling that we can protect what the other is as other nor prepare the path going to meet with them.

• Our tradition, founded upon the intelligibility, the mastery, the unveiling for us of that which is, has prevented the approach to the other through gestures and words that disturb the entering into presence with him, or her. The other cannot be reduced to a substratum starting from which we elaborate our own culture, whatever its nature would be. The other is the one toward whom we advance in darkness, the disclosure of their coming never being revealed in the light of day. Nor does the memory of the other amount to that of a thing which can remain immutably tied to a word. It is rather a question of remembering a living being, multiple in what it is and still in becoming. The other is not comparable to a simple being standing in front of us, and that we have to integrate into the whole of our world thanks to a name. The other goes against this univocal appellation, this integration into a whole that is not proper to them, unless their otherness is lost. Thus, it is to what the other says that we have to listen and not only to the language spoken, to which the other would co-belong with me, with us – in a same logos, a same logic. These speak to us starting from the perspective on the Being of a subject who is neither universal nor neuter. To integrate or homologate the other into such a point of view amounts to destroying alterity. Now it is on such a condition that our tradition claims to be able to hear and even understand the other, which means not to listen to this other.

Wisdom, according to us, would be to renounce difference in order to find an agreement in sameness. But such a same is, in a way, already a nullification of the living becoming of whoever speaks and of him, or her, to whom it is spoken. A relinquishing also of the fecundity of a dialogue, of what it presupposes as perpetual creation, which cannot be said or memorized once and for all in appropriate forms.

The same goes for the other. To claim to safeguard the other thanks to a definitive status in our memory amounts to remembering something, and not to preparing a place in which someone would be preserved. Here there is neither any word which could evoke in a lasting way, nor any decisive integration into a whole, nor any irrevocable unveiling. It is in the respect of a mystery that we preserve in us for them that the other might take shelter. In a place which does not claim a light without shadow, an identity without becoming, an immutable space. The other in us must remain flesh, living, moving. Not transformed into some idea, no matter how ideal. Not reduced to some sleep, more or less lethal. Nor brought back to a natural immediacy that we would not yet have cultivated in ourselves. One might as well say not assimilated in some way to us, including through the mediation of a supposed sameness.

The Name of the Other

The rift between the other and me is irreducible. To be sure we can build bridges, join our energies, feast and celebrate encounters, but the union is never definitive, on pain of no longer existing. Union implies returning into oneself, moving away, dissenting, separating. To correspond with one's own becoming requires an alternation of approaching the other and dividing from him, or her. This must not be understood as a simple controversy to be reduced to the same. Difference demands rather the relinquishing of the whole, whether this be in oneself or with the other, and of what would maintain the illusion that it could or ought to be reached. Fidelity to oneself and to the other requires abandoning the lure of an immediate fullness in order to obtain sometimes another one, the fruit of an encounter that it would be fitting to celebrate and remember without wanting it to be permanent or at the disposal of one person alone.

To fix such a fullness in a decisive manner amounts to reducing it to death more than to keeping it as something still to germinate. It would be the same if the link with the other were integrated, once and for all, into a whole supposed to guarantee an availability thanks to the logos. The space kept free for approaching is then already filled, and the approach becomes impossible, except in a fictive way and in the name of an unconscious bondage to a common death.

Some lightning strike of love will be necessary, some flash or illumination in order to reopen the path of proximity. But such fulguration is not easily shared and it would be less indispensable if the other was listened to every day in their difference. To enter into presence then takes on another meaning.

A single Whole cannot hold together everyone and everything. It is, in fact, difficult to shelter another in one's own house, among others that of language. Except for a moment and with the consciousness that this is the case. A home needs to be appropriate to the one who dwells in it – it is the place of preservation of one's own intimacy. Which has more in common with a nocturnal touching than with lightning. And that the logos or a God, such as Zeus, might rigidify through an envelope, breaking off the porosity of touch, if not consuming life itself. A subject is not an object or a thing, and it does not suffice to name it in order to designate what is proper to it and to permit this subject to be present. Unless we confuse naming and calling out, and we assimilate, this time, the cry or evocation of the name with what makes the other arrive, mentally or physically, in representation or in reality. Of which other is it then a question? An animal? A slave? One who is subjugated, in any case.

To the call of their name, the other, if they remain free and faithful to themselves, will respond with a gathering of self rather than with an availability to the gaze or the hand. The other as other never appears, and especially not thanks to a designation by a name. Rather this is what makes the other withdraw into their self. Unless the other renounces to be, so as to get caught for or by an other. Appearing then becomes a way of being possessed through the gaze.

God, in this sense, really represents the transfer of the other into the beyond. As invisible, he acts as guarantor of alterity as such. To be sure, some of his predicates identify him as the God of a people, of a tradition or culture corresponding to a part of the world, to a stage of History – a then less absolute representation of the other as such. But a God who keeps his freedom in spite of our call, except sometimes because of compassion, a God who escapes our gaze and our hold, truly seems to be the guarantor of the memory that the other exists. God is waiting for our encountering and entering into relation with him, or her. God is a beyond with regard to our discoveries and homologations, cultivations and fabrications, reductions to the One and to the same, where energy of or for the other is used without recognizing their irreducible emergence.

Emergence from the logos as well. The other cannot be already said by the saying, and neither can the other represent the whole of the saying. Except their own – never absolute nor definitive. If it is imagined as an equivalent of the logos, the name of God still designates that of a subject capable of producing and mastering language. But either he tolerates other Gods, masters of other languages or words – organized differently or expressing a diverse reality – or such a God becomes the place of the annihilation of real alterity. A place of projection of a desire of or for the other which is suspended there in order to not be accomplished. Retaining in himself the attraction to the other, God then risks hardening the borders between cultures which do not share the same divine representations and abolishing the differences between subjects belonging to the same tradition.

God, as the absolutely other, also allows excesses in the present, without assessing the difference between the other and me. Paradoxically, the one to whom man has entrusted the authority over him and the care of being his master becomes the source of the authority and the mastery of man over the other, over the world. Containing in himself both the Same and the Other, God has in some way abolished the yardstick of any measure, in particular of speaking, but also of making. Left to his excessive tendencies, man then proceeds by dazzling revelations, advanced by leaps and bounds which extend over the other and over the world the net of a final revelation, of a last flash of lightning. Light and action, not limited by the real existence and the Being of the other and of the world, become little by little concealed in a lack of differentiation of thinking, a paralysis of the gesture.

That the word keep its mystery, very well, but that it dispossess the other of their own, no. And that thought results from a reflection never said between thinking and thought perhaps corresponds to an intuition worthy of contemplation. But it thus remains solipsistic. And would it not be fitting to find for it a site built while taking into account the respect of the other as other? Which complicates things a little. Because, in what a Heidegger names the "fold," the fact that the other cannot be contained in the one should now intervene, which prevents closing the fold in the same.

Open, is it still a fold? How, from then on, to speak about the place where thinking is at work? Listening to the present speaking of the other and to the response to provide assumes a new importance here. It is no longer a matter of receiving, alone or as a people, the gift of a constituted speech but of being attentive to what the other says, or wants to say, including in his, or her, silences. What some would assign to a secondary discipline, such as psychology, merits being considered as a fundamental dimension of thinking. Its methods thus find themselves profoundly modified. For example, it is not because of my speech that the other exists or is. Even if my speaking can bring a surplus of existence, the other does not receive who they are univocally from my speech, even if I were God. And the other's appearing is not solely dependent upon what I know of them. Besides the fact that what I know of the other remains partial, such a knowledge is always already in the past, foreign to the core of Being from which the other draws the organization of the becoming of their existence, thus of entering into presence in the present. Confining him, or her, in a past perception, I have already covered the other with a shroud, embalmed, entombed, evoked the other as living without respecting their life.

It is not simply through being named that the other will be preserved. To renounce saying the other while respecting their transcendence safeguards the other more as other. If, in some manner, this guarding could be considered as a fold, the fold would be silent. But this representation of a method is perhaps not suitable. It still evokes too much the autistic mastery of a subject. Taking account of the transcendence of the other in thinking amounts rather to a releasing all hold that sends each one back to what or who he, or she, is. A sort of giving oneself up to earth, even to sky, a sort of returning to the real starting from which the world will continue to be elaborated without ever being closed in a whole. Always and still to be built and to be thought. Always and still open for a dialogue with the other.

Which makes perception an act other than seizing, naming, reproducing. Then looking and listening apprehend the other without their appearing being determined by a pre-established presence. In the chiasmus between seeing and hearing, a presence unfolds that I could not anticipate through a logos already existing for me, nor in the absolute. The attentive approach to the other gives me a real and a meaning still to come and unknown for me. They appear to me thanks to the withdrawal of the other in their self and my withdrawal in my self. This gesture does not exclude but accompanies the opening to the other. The truth that discloses itself in this way is related to the moment of the encounter, its light keeping a human measure. It is only bestowed thanks to a fidelity of each to oneself.

From the other irradiates a truth which we can receive without its source being visible. That from which the other elaborates meaning remains a mystery for us but we can indirectly perceive something of it. Such an operation transforms the subject, enlightens the subject in a way that is both visible and invisible. The light that then reaches us illuminates the world otherwise, and discloses to us the particularity of our point of view. It says nothing in a way, pronounces no word but makes clear the limits of a horizon, of a site of thinking, of existing, of Being. It opens new possibilities of perceiving and of elaborating space and time, delivering them from the opacity of the night while still arranging nothing – only the unfolding of another manner of looking at, of listening to, of welcoming the real, taking into account the importance of the other in their existence. It keeps alive the astonishment, the questioning, the movement of thinking and of saying.

These no longer seek in death the shelter to secure their dwelling. A fidelity to life and to what life requires as daily work of elaboration, of becoming, of cultivation permits them to survive and to unfold. In such an operation assured by each one, life itself becomes light, brightness necessary for an encounter which cannot occur in the horizon of death. Death, in fact, is always one's own whatever may be the destiny of mortals shared by those who draw near to one another. It is rather life which can provide for a place where the two can approach, welcome, gather one another in the respect of their alterity, of their difference.

Without a cultivation of life, no encounter or dialogue is possible between living beings. But this has been unrecognized, forgotten. And where we could give to one another a way both for becoming and dwelling, we have neglected this resource, taking as a partner the frozen, the defined, the dead rather than the living. Playing some games perhaps, but alone. Without moving on the way thanks to the light of what we receive from the other, as well as in response to our own gifts. Provided that we ourselves do not throw light on the other only with our words but accept letting the other be, the irradiation that emanates from him, or her, can guide us.

It is not we who can impart to the other appearing, we can hardly do it for things. Silencing what we already know is often more useful in order to let the other appear, and light ourselves up through this entry into presence irreducible to our knowledge.

Such excess with respect to the other's self-affection and to my own self-affection opens a place where we can unveil ourselves to one another while remaining hidden, sheltered by our proximity with ourselves. Which never comes to light except indirectly through how it transforms our own appearing. This non-appearing of proximity does not correspond to a lack which it would be fitting to remedy. It belongs to proximity to never give itself to be seen. For that, it has probably been little cultivated in our tradition.

This Nothingness Which Separates Us

In our culture gathering oneself is not secured in proportion to opening oneself to. No doubt, for the human subject, this gesture is more difficult than for certain flowers. But would not a human have over them the advantage of being able to provide for an opening and a gathering in a free and decided manner? For this to be so, it would be necessary that language not hold the human artificially open, cut off from its reserve of life. But also that the human subject really be two, and that the respect of the difference between the two assure or reinforce the pulsating movement between the opening and the withdrawal. Already determined by cosmic rhythms – night or day, light or dark, cold or hot... – the rhythm marking the times of opening and closing would be redoubled thanks to the respect for every living being considered as such, and punctuated, a third time, by the relation with the other as a living subject different from me.

In this place, the scansion opening/closing is most truly adjusted in order to safeguard natural and spiritual life. Such a gesture cannot be defined in a simply abstract way once and for all. It requires an adjustment to the concrete situation of the encounter and to the being of each one. It also needs *philia*, love or friendship for the other, which agrees to renounce appropriation without limits in order to let this other be.

It is not only the act of speaking that allows the human subject to attain this third level of opening/closing up again. Speech moreover has often served to prevent the human subject from doing it. The ability to desire and to love without being subjected to one's instincts is more decisive here. As is the capacity to go out from the same, to not be coiled up in the proper, to recognize difference – with what it implies about the practice of negativity –, which permits a movement and a passage from the heart to thinking, from friendship to listening, from speaking of to speaking with. These dimensions make the human a living being truly other with respect to the animal, which is more enclosed within one world.

In the dialogue between two different subjects, nihilism finds a positive fulfillment. Calling into question one's own world so as to bring about the existence and the access to the world of the other allows and needs the place of the nothing as a possible articulation of one world with the other. This no longer anything of one's own and nothing yet in common calls into question the values of a subject, not toward a destruction without any tomorrow but with a view toward the construction of a future in which the human will find its most perfect blossoming.

• The practice of the negative here is insurmountable in an absolute subjectivity or an absolute objectivity. It is what safeguards the unappropriable site of difference – the fact that the other will never be I, nor me, nor mine. Instead of working toward the realization of a world of one's own, the use of the negative serves to maintain an insurmountable place between two subjects. In order to meet with the other, I must first let be, even restore, the nothing that separates us. It is a negative path which leads to the approach of the different and the possible relation with him, or with her. I am not you and you will forever remain other to me, such is the necessary presupposition for the entering into presence of the one and the other, of the one with the other. The search for a link requires the respect for the strangeness of the one to the other, the recognition of a nothing in common calling into question the proper of each one. •

In this sense, nihilism no longer rests on a new border that we would or would not have to cross. The nothing lies in a real that has always been. What being is in its reality compels us to the questioning of values that Nietzsche calls for as the challenging of our tradition and a possible access to a new epoch of thinking.

The coming of a presence that shines no longer belongs only to the world. Consciousness, not as a simple knowledge of nature, of things, of objects, but as knowledge of oneself and of the other, going as far as to respect the unknowable and the mystery, becomes the chance for an entering into presence that has not yet occurred: that of the human as such. The light that then shines is that of an intimate sun which supports life and makes it grow without illuminating it with a diurnal light.

Consciousness nevertheless is awake, attentive to the measure of the territory proper to each one. The gaze turns around toward the interior, illuminating the flesh and illuminated by it. It was a means of more or less abstract distanciation, it becomes an irradiation of the intimate to which it gives a nocturnal perspective upon itself. And also upon that which surrounds, that of which the approach is perceived, which it is fitting to welcome and also to restore in its place. Illumination does not separate from the discreet warmth of friendship, of love, that delimits the site of dwelling around its hearth.

To this hearth the link with each one, with each thing returns, for the estimation of its place in the whole. Which is not determined by a simple apprehension by the mental nor by the call or recall of a name.

Presence is no longer at our disposal. It exists and grows from an autonomous life. The approach of which requires both caring and letting be. It is not a question here of shaping the other in accordance with an intention of one's own, be it that of situating the other in the whole of a world. If we have to shape someone in this sense, it is rather ourselves, not without attending to the irreducible contribution that we can and must give to a whole that is already there. The same goes for the other as well – what the other has singularly to offer must be heard before imagining the place that, for the time being, we can grant to the other in a whole.

The harmony of a world organized beforehand can govern neither the relation to oneself nor the relation to the other. They must emerge from it on pain of not being. Listening to oneself and to the other needs a still virgin place, from which to receive the speaking which comes from a new presence and to prepare for the fecundity of its advent in the future. The unity and the movement of the world will no longer result from the homologation in the same but from a relation in which difference remains the condition of presence and the source of becoming. Where it was a matter of integrating into the same, it is now a question of recognizing what differs, and of trying to compose a moving whole in which each one welcomes the contribution of the other while guarding their own life.

To be calm and to be changing must harmoniously come together in a dwelling that will not be inertia but a becoming in faithfulness, to oneself and to the other. Each one provides the other with the confirmation of a limit without imposing upon the other any form. Rather this form will arise thanks to the return to the world proper to a subjectivity.

To give, from the outside, a mould in which to pour oneself or to which to conform cannot correspond to the efflorescence of a form of one's own. To be sure objective supports exist to favor or to respect the blossoming of such a form: linguistic or legal frameworks, for example, but also environments for living, like architecture. But they serve to aid and to protect, not to submit growth to a definitive imprint. Rather, they are supports of the horizon, which cannot stand in the heart of the subject itself, preventing this heart from beating with the rhythm of life. The objectivity on which they propose modeling oneself does not substitute for the objectivity of a subjectivity irreducible to another. It concerns another level.

Thus what appeared as a priori, even transcendence, in relation to the unfolding of a subjectivity, becomes a piece of the assembly that was useful for the elaboration or the comprehension of this subjectivity at a moment of History. A historical configuration cannot prevent the present Being or the becoming of the subject through the imposition of its imprint, without leading to a more or less totalitarian authoritarianism.

But whence comes the fact that suffering has so often been associated with form? Would this not be tied to the solitude of a man who claims, all alone, to construct and build the world? If form also results from the other, from the friendship that is felt toward the other and from the friendship that he, or she, offers, is its efflorescence not also happiness? Does the acceptance of a limit, of a not being the whole, necessarily imply grief? Or does it engender suffering only because of a mental pretension founded upon the forgetting of what brings felicity? Founded as well upon the forgetting of faithfulness to life, whose guarding and growth are accompanied by happiness, even if they require discipline and renunciation.

Whoever knows the gathering together into the most intimate only through suffering, does not know the illuminating grace of love. This also, thanks to another light than that cultivated by our metaphysics, opens a place of resource and of meditative gathering. It implies, it is true, the ability to let be as much as to make. And the acceptance of a sharing between shadow and light.

Light never illuminates the whole, without paralyzing becoming. It uncovers, for a moment, a figure of the whole. This emerges according to the perspective from which it is envisaged. Its return into the darkness comes from the fact that it is considered differently and also that it is situated differently in the whole – the whole of the world but also the whole of humanity insomuch as humans turn back to themselves, attentive to their own interiority as a space inside and outside the whole.

The human has to turn not only toward the outside but also toward the inside, on pain of losing its humanity. And a human's making cannot be only exterior, it is also interior. The matter that it works on is not simply other than human, it is also itself. Surpassing the matter that it is in view of its nullification should not be a human's undertaking, but rather transforming this matter so far as to make it a work of art, to transubstantiate it into a more subtle, spiritual, even divine, matter. To illuminate it so that it enlightens he, or she, who gazes upon it, who contemplates it.

The light that someone radiates is not necessarily perceived as such by the one who gives it to be seen. Perhaps it grants the peace that whoever dwells in oneself experiences. And, with it, the joy. A proof that mortals are destined for light, but a light often visible through its effects rather than in itself. And which lights up the night while letting it rest in darkness. Without violating the calm of such a shelter, of which touch perhaps safeguards the protection. Touch which lies invisible in everything, including seeing. Touch which will remain hidden in what is most tactile in it. And which will want to impose borders in order to be forgotten in what it illuminates beyond the appearing of forms.

Touch which allows turning back to oneself, in the dwelling of an intimate light. But which also goes to encounter the other, illuminated-illuminating, overflowing one's own world in order to taste another brightness. In order to give and to receive what can enlighten mortals on their path.

Which man has often dismissed to the benefit of a God, whose light would also radiate in the night. Provided however that he resist the dominance of the light of our so-called reason, that he remain faithful to his invisibility for the eyes of mortals. Faithful in some way to the Nothingness that he should guarantee. A Nothingness which is not nothing.